HOW TO BE A MONASTIC
and Not Leave Your Day Job

A VOICE FROM THE MONASTERY

HOW TO BE A MONASTIC
and Not Leave Your Day Job

An Invitation to Oblate Life

Brother Benet Tvedten OSB

PARACLETE PRESS
BREWSTER, MASSACHUSETTS

2006   First Printing

Copyright © 2006 by Br. Benet Tvedten
ISBN 1-55725-449-4

All quotes from St. Benedict's Rule are taken from *The Rule of St. Benedict in English*, edited by Timothy Fry, OSB. Copyright 1981 by the Order of St. Benedict, Inc. Published by The Liturgical Press, Collegeville, Minnesota. Reprinted with permission.

Library of Congress Cataloging–in–Publication Data

Tvedten, Benet.
    How to be a monastic and not leave your day job : an invitation to oblate life / Benet Tvedten.
       p.   cm.
    ISBN 1–55725–449–4
    1. Third orders. 2. Benedictines—Spiritual life. I. Title.
    BX2840.T84   2006
    255'.093—dc22   2005026917

10 9 8 7 6 5 4 3 2 1

Published by Paraclete Press
Brewster, Massachusetts
www.paracletepress.com
Printed in the United States of America.

Dedicated to all Oblates and Oblate Directors,
present, past. and future and especially to

—Sister Jean Frances Dolan, OSB

CONTENTS

I began thinking I would read an historic document of great interest. Quickly that element vanished and I became absorbed so totally that even as I turned the pages, I knew that the man who picked that book up early on a cold winter's afternoon at the Abbey of Solesmes would never again be the same. Every line permeated me, like the odor of fresh-baked bread. Benedict radiated a warmth and a health of soul that united me in affection to him forever.

—John Howard Griffin
Upon reading the *Rule of St. Benedict* for the first time

Introduction

JUST AS WE BEGAN THE CEREMONY IN HER LIVING ROOM, THE PHONE RANG. "I can't talk now," Frances said. "I'm becoming a Benedictine." She hung up, and we resumed the rite of oblation in which Frances promised "to serve God and all people according to the Rule of St. Benedict." She was in her seventies then, and had been confined to a wheelchair with muscular dystrophy since the age of four. Ordinarily, oblation is made at the monastery where a person has chosen to affiliate. Frances Schmidt, however, had no way of getting to Blue Cloud Abbey near Marvin in northeastern South Dakota, where I live. I had invested her a year before when she and her sister were at the abbey. Rather than wait for an opportunity to make oblation in the presence of the abbot and the monastic community, she was eager to do so when I informed her that I would be able to stop by her home in Dell Rapids while on my way to Sioux Falls.

Nowadays, the terms "lay monk" and "the new monk" are in common usage. Does this convey to us canonically professed monks and nuns that we're all washed up? This much I know: The number of oblates everywhere keeps growing and growing. When the oblates gather here for a monthly meeting, there is not enough room for everyone in the choir stalls. We have to go down into the nave of the church to sing vespers. When dinner is served, the oblates occupy the tables in the monastery refectory, and most of the monks go to the guest dining room.

The following people were all invested as oblates at Blue Cloud in one recent calendar year: a schoolteacher and his wife from Wyoming, a truck driver from Montana, a Catholic priest from North Dakota, a Lutheran pastor from South Dakota, a retreatant who'd come here from Colorado, a student at Augustana (a Lutheran college in Sioux Falls), a seminarian from the Baptist seminary in the same city, a housewife from across the border in Ortonville, Minnesota, and a dental surgeon from Sioux Falls. Why are people from various places and professions so eager to become Oblates of St. Benedict? The Reverend Dennis Okholm, a Presbyterian minister and theology professor, who is an oblate of my community, explains why he and others come to us from different religious backgrounds: "From the time of my initial visit to Blue Cloud Abbey, I began exploring Benedictine spirituality and its roots. It does not take long before one begins to realize the significant place that the Rule of Benedict and its author have had in the history of Christianity—a significance enhanced by the fact that Benedict, like Augustine, belongs to the entire Christian church, for he came long before the Roman Catholic–Protestant split and centuries before the final and formal East-West division."

Father Edward Vebelun, a monk of St. John's Abbey, Collegeville, Minnesota, surveyed forty-five men and women oblate directors in the spring of 2004. They reported having a total of 8,915 oblates affiliated with their monasteries, while there were only 2,872 vowed Benedictines, male and female, in these same monasteries.

What are they seeking—Frances Schmidt and all the many others who have become Oblates of St. Benedict? Father Edward found that the oblate directors agreed on several attractions. First, the monastic community's support is an attraction—having a group of monks or nuns praying for oblates. The values taught by Benedictines are appealing and so is their structured prayer life. These directors are convinced that becoming an oblate is a means of spiritual renewal for many people.

In the year 2000, Sister Antoinette Purcell, the oblate director of Our Lady of Grace Monastery in Beech Grove, Indiana, was the moderator for a panel of oblates at the American Benedictine Academy Convention. The theme that year was "Reading the Signs of the Times: The Good News of Monastic Life." Although the number of oblates is increasing and fewer men and women are being drawn to the vowed Benedictine life, Sister Antoinette believes the good news is that we all have a purpose. "Together we can be one voice that speaks of how to be in relation to self, God, and others just by being who we are called to be in the place where we are."

This book attempts to explain the calling of an Oblate of St. Benedict. I have been my community's oblate director for almost thirty years, and I know many other oblates because of my involvement with the North American Association of Benedictine Oblate Directors. Two oblates per community attend the Association's biennial meeting, and they always outnumber the directors who are present. I have also met other oblates by conducting retreats for them at the monasteries where they are affiliated. Oblates are my kind of people!

Although Benedict's Rule—a prologue and seventy-three short chapters—was written for monks at Monte Cassino in sixth-century Italy, in a few centuries nuns also began following the Rule as a guide to Christian living. All of us—monks, nuns, and oblates—are Benedictine.

"Listen" is the first word of the Rule, as Benedict invites us to follow his manner of Christian life. Listen to him with "the ear of your heart," he says. "This is advice from a father who loves you; welcome it, and faithfully put it into practice" (Prologue:1).

Benedict Lives Today

Benedict lived at the end of the classical age when Roman civilization had been overrun by the barbarian tribes. It was Benedict's monastic sons and daughters who, in the words of Pope Paul VI, "brought Christian culture to the peoples scattered from the Mediterranean to Scandinavia, from Ireland to Poland." In 1964, Paul VI proclaimed St. Benedict the patron of Europe. In a time called the Dark Ages, Benedictines taught people how to read and write, to cultivate the soil, to develop crafts and the arts, and to pray. Pope Paul's *Proclamation of St. Benedict as Patron of All Europe* stated that through the law of Christ Benedict "brought stability and development to public and private institutions."

Charlemagne, the Holy Roman Emperor, was a great promoter of Benedictine monastic life. He had been illiterate until he put a monk in charge of the palace school. Charlemagne himself became one of Alcuin's students. By the twelfth century, Benedict's was the principal rule followed by monks and nuns in Europe. Although the nobility founded many monastic houses in order to have the assurance that someone would pray for them, everyone in the realm benefited from the works of the Benedictines.

Besides offering hospitality to travelers and pilgrims, the monastery provided welfare assistance. A monastic official called the almoner offered food, clothing, and financial help to needy persons who came to the monastery for help.

Farming methods were developed by the Benedictines, and they constructed roads and bridges in order to take their crops and produce to market. The orchards of Europe were first planted by monks and nuns. Vineyards were tended in monasteries as far north as England.

There was a need to produce books from which the monks and nuns prayed in common, and books for the students they taught. Books were needed for libraries and for new monastic houses. Scribes copied books in the scriptorium, and decorators and illuminators embellished them. "Their vigor saved the classical works of the ancients," Paul VI acknowledged in his 1964 decree, "and transmitted them to posterity, and restored culture at a time when the humanistic patrimony and the arts of civilization were about to be lost."

Pope Paul referred to the spiritual unity that the "faithful followers of their great master" created in the Middle Ages, and then asked for St. Benedict's intercession in our era. Many people today have become disciples of this same

Benedict, Abbot of Monte Cassino, whose sixth-century Rule for monks has brought meaning to their own lives. Dr. Janet Buchanan, whose doctoral thesis is on the Oblates of St. Benedict, speaking at a conference of the North American Association of Oblate Directors, told them, "When an individual reaches the point where he or she can say what I want most in life is to be a monk, then the way is open to a whole new stage of living. Benedictinism lives in individuals who are Benedictine, and not necessarily in monasteries." The Reverend Patrick Henry, theologian and ecumenist, says, "There's hope when the old St. Benedict is seen new and afresh."

A few years before his death in 1999, Cardinal Basil Hume, who was then the Archbishop of Westminster, spoke to Parliament about the relevance St. Benedict's Rule has in modern life. "The Rule of St. Benedict reminds us that a sense of community has to be created and constantly worked at. Calls for social cohesion will fall on deaf ears if we see ourselves as a collection of individuals, rather than as a society of people with a shared interest in each other's welfare."

This certainly relates to what Benedict says in his chapter on good zeal. "No one is to pursue what he judges better for himself, but instead, what he judges better for someone else" (72:7). Although Benedict realized there were special needs for particular people such as the young and the aged, he did not cater to special interest groups that were selfish and exclusive. An abbot, he says, "is to show equal love to everyone." An abbot must work for the good of the whole community, the entire family.

St. Benedict's monasteries are open to all of humanity. All guests are to be received as Christ Himself. The monastic community is to welcome them with "the courtesy of love" (53:3). The same year that Cardinal Hume addressed the Members of Parliament he also spoke to an assembly of English Roman Catholics. He told them: "Our reaction to other persons, especially those with whom we do not agree, ought always to be characterized by a willingness to show respect; to be careful not to damage another person's good name; to affirm what is good in another; never to be rude and insulting. The spirit of the Pharisees lurks in each one of us, tempting us to sit in judgment on others and even to seek to exclude them from the church."

Benedict wants us to show respect for one another. He teaches us to have reverence. There is so much irreverence in the world these days. It seems so many Christians are in a state of conflict. We say such hateful things about one another and to one another. Esther de Waal believes the language of the Rule resonates today "with many people who are on the edge of the church, who are questioning and seeking. They find many things in the institutional church difficult, but they still find a deep longing in themselves."

Our new pope took the name of Benedict. A lot of people are saying he chose that name because St. Benedict lived in a time like our own—a time, they say, when civilization had collapsed. Benedict and his followers brought about its restoration. Benedict was a man of peace. Today's pope—Benedict XVI—would like to restore peace among those of us in his fold, and like the earlier Benedict, he wants to extend hospitality to the whole world. On the day of Pope Benedict's inauguration, he declared in his homily that in his governance he would be careful to listen. *Listen*—that first word of the Rule of Benedict. The monk is to listen to the abbot, the abbot is to listen to the monks, and the monks are to listen to one another. This too is the courtesy of love.

"My real program of governance is not to do my own will, not to pursue my own ideas, but to listen, together with the whole church." These words of Pope Benedict XVI recall what St. Benedict says regarding someone who has been chosen abbot. "Let him recognize that his goal must be profit for the monks, not preeminence for himself" (64:8).

In 1991 the Abbot Primate of the Benedictine Order, Viktor Dammertz, asked, "How does one explain the general applicability of Benedict's Rule?" This question was posed in an address regarding the Oblates of St. Benedict presented to the monastic superiors of the United Kingdom and Ireland. "I believe a point should be made here which cannot be stressed too strongly. Benedict did not write his rule for an elite group. What he wrote was a rather small rule for beginners who are on the way toward

Christian perfection. He wanted to teach his monks how to lead at least a half-way respectable life in which they would perform the usual, everyday things well."

Being Benedictine—a monastic or an oblate—means trying a little harder to show the courtesy of love for one another, to see Christ in the people with whom we live, work, and pray—and to look for Him even in the people with whom we disagree.

The Rule has endured because it was written for people who want to dwell together in unity in the midst of their diversity. It was written for people who want to be family, community.

Oblates of St. Benedict are Christians from various families and backgrounds who have come together to form a covenant with the monastic community of their affiliation. In Benedict's day, a classless society was something out of the ordinary. Romans, former slaves, and barbarians all came to live in Benedict's monastery under his rule. Benedict does not ask monks for mere toleration of one another. "To their fellow monks they show the pure love of brothers" (72:8), he says. They are all one in Christ.

The goal of Benedictine life is presented in the Prologue to the Rule. Benedict asks, "What . . . is more delightful than this voice of the Lord calling to us? See how the Lord in his love shows us the way of life." Oblates of St. Benedict have responded to this voice that has called out to them.

St. Odo, who became the Abbot of the great French Abbey of Cluny in 927, said the praises of St. Benedict are sung among all tribes, nations, and tongues. Benedict has drawn followers of both sexes and all ages and from many different places, and all of them are "looking up to him, as though he were present." Odo believes there will be great joy when all of us have reached the end of the journey mapped out for us by Benedict. After seeing us assembled in heaven, Benedict will be so happy that he'll dance.

PART ONE

St. Benedict and Benedictine Spirituality

What is Benedictine Spirituality?

A WOMAN WHO ONCE INQUIRED ABOUT BECOMING AN OBLATE WAS TOLD THAT THIS MEANT THE OFFERING OF ONE'S SELF. "I'd rather offer myself to Christ," she told me, "than to St. Benedict." She was right. Benedict admonishes all of us who follow his rule to offer ourselves to Christ. In the Prologue, we are encouraged "to do battle for the true King, Christ the Lord" (Pro. 3). At the end of the Rule, he says, "Let [us] prefer nothing whatever to Christ, and may he bring us all together to everlasting life" (72:11-12).

The entire Rule of St. Benedict is centered on Christ and the Christian life. That's why everyone—not just monks and nuns—can benefit from following it. Benedict added nothing new to Christian doctrine. He preached gospel values applied in an orderly fashion to everyday life. His way of living is similar to that of the early Christians who are described in the Acts of the Apostles. They devoted themselves to holding all things in common, breaking bread together, and praising the Lord. Benedict is focused on Christ in prayer, work, and in familial relationships. Seek Christ, Benedict insists, but he realizes that you don't have to go very far to find Him. His image is reflected in ourselves and in everyone else.

St. Gregory the Great tells of a hermit named Martin whose foot was bound by a chain fastened to a rock. When Benedict heard of this, he sent one of his monks to tell Martin that he should be bound to Christ instead of a chain of iron.

Christ is the chain that binds us, and we are all bound to one another. We live our common calling in community, in family. Benedictine spirituality is not just "Jesus and me." It's the two of us and everybody else in whom Jesus is present—the people with whom I live and work, the people to whom I'm related by blood, and those for whom I have a responsibility.

The stranger, the newcomer—welcome them also as Christ, Benedict says. Benedict teaches all of us how to live together, how to get along with each other regardless of our differences. Benedict calls his community a school of the Lord's service. He wants us to learn from one another. He also refers to his community as a workshop where we use the tools of good works. These are the Ten Commandments and the teachings of Jesus. The asceticism under which we live is "nothing harsh, nothing burdensome" (Pro.:46). Although burdens may enter our lives, we aren't to go looking for them, or to create them for ourselves. Moderation and balance, even in the saving of our souls, constitute the ascetical life prescribed by Benedict. But if we do find this life difficult in the beginning, he guarantees this in the Prologue of the Rule: "as we progress in this way of life and in faith, we shall run on the path of God's com-mandments, our hearts overflowing with the inexpressible delight of love" (Pro.:49). The Rule helps us to avoid certain things we might stumble over while on our way through life.

Some ascetics before Benedict's time appear to us now as having been rather extreme in their practices. Martin, the hermit whom Benedict corrected, was clinging to an outdated and excessive form of eremitical asceticism. He was following in the tradition of chain wearers like St. Sabinas who was so weighted down that he had to walk on all fours. Martin, of course, couldn't walk far from the rock to which his foot was attached. Another desert monk, instead of wearing chains, bound himself with the root of an oak tree. Alcoholics Anonymous would call that "looking for an easier, softer way." There were also browsers who went around the desert searching for patches of grass to eat, and statics who stood perfectly still for days at a time, and even slept while upright. The stylites perched in trees or built towers on which to sit—far removed from society. Perhaps the most famous of them was Symeon, who remained on top of his thirty-foot column near Antioch for more than three decades. Benedict lived as a hermit for three years, but he abandoned this life style for the communal living. However, he did not embrace any established rule that had been written specifically for monks who lived in community.

Scholars now believe that Benedict, in writing his famous rule, adapted an earlier text called *The Rule of the Master*, written near Rome at the end of the fifth century. The Master portrays himself as a grouch. He is everything Benedict says an abbot should not be. The Master's Rule is indeed harsh and burdensome. The crotchety old abbot does not have much confidence in his monks, and is constantly suspicious of them. If the brothers say they are sick and unable to get out of bed and work, the Master advises that they be given "only liquids and eggs or warm water, which the really sick can hardly get down, so that if they are pretending hunger, at least this will force them to get up" (RM 69:2-3). In contrast, Benedict says the sick are to be treated as Christ would be treated. Although monks should

6

not make unnecessary demands on their caregivers, Benedict does not presume that any monk will fake poor health. The Rule of the Master makes the monk who has aches and pains, but no fever, go to church at the scheduled times. "And if he cannot stand, let him chant the psalms lying on a mat . . . But let the brother standing next to him keep an eye of him so he does not go to sleep" (RM 69:10-11).

Benedict cut out large sections of the Master's Rule and eliminated other parts all together. He tempered his monastic rule with more moderate and compassionate admonitions. His monks obeyed out of love rather than for fear of a wrathful master. Benedict is obviously more understanding and forgiving of his monks' imperfections than the Master is of his. Benedict clearly states in the last chapter of his rule that it has been written to show that we have achieved "some degree of virtue." It is a rule for "beginners" (73:1), he says.

Benedict's abbot listens to the community and says even the junior monks must attend community or chapter meetings because "the Lord often reveals what is better to the younger." Benedict wants to hear from everyone. He is no doubt willing also to listen to the voices of those who disagree with him. The Master will hear only from those whom he designates to speak.

Because the Rule of St. Benedict is a sixth-century document, some of its legislation is no longer applicable. Benedict himself realized that not everything from the past could be applied in his time. The matter of drinking wine is often offered as an example. "We read that monks should not drink wine at all, but since the monks of our day cannot be convinced of this, let us at least agree to drink moderately, and not to the point of excess" (40:6). Benedict says it's all right to bend rules. He bent the Master's Rule all out of shape, and allowed for making exceptions to his own rules.

I remind the oblates that it's much easier being a disciple of Benedict than being guided by the Rule of the Master. "Wouldn't you rather be an oblate of St. Benedict instead of an oblate of the Master?" I ask them. Benedict has designed his rule for Christian living so that both the strong and the weak may live side by side. Following the Rule of Benedict is not like taking on a religion separate from the one to which a person already belongs. Oblates aren't re-baptized. Benedict, in his Prologue, refers to us as having been counted as children of God now, and he speaks, of "his good gifts which are [already] in us" (Pro.:6).

Following the Rule as an Oblate of St. Benedict is a method of seeking God through what is familiar and by rather ordinary means. John McQuiston II, a lawyer and lay leader in his Episcopal parish, has paraphrased the Rule of St. Benedict in a little book called *Always We Begin Again*. In his introduction, he writes: "The Rule teaches that if we take control of our lives, if we are intentional and careful in how we spend the hours of each irreplaceable day, if we discipline ourselves to live in a balanced and thankful way, we will create from our experiences, whatever they may be, the best possible life. Surely this knowledge is as invaluable now as it was in the sixth century."

The Benedictine manner is ordinary. Some people are disappointed when they discover monks and nuns are common, ordinary people. This is why it is easy to identify with us and with what St. Benedict teaches us. We all belong to a family of one sort or another. We're taught how to live in this family, loving and supporting one another, even those of us who are most difficult to love and support. We learn patience from St. Benedict. We benefit from the patience of a saint.

A Life of Prayer

Benedict encourages good zeal but advises against becoming zealots. Moderation should be our aim in everything—from the amount of food and drink we consume to the number of psalms we pray. "Prayer should therefore be short and pure, unless perhaps it is prolonged under the inspiration of divine grace." He is speaking of private prayer here. "In community, however, prayer should always be brief; and when the superior gives the signal, all should rise together" (20:4-5).

Again Benedict considers the times in which he is living. After providing a structure for communal prayer, he says that a community that is dissatisfied with this arrangement may do it some other way, providing that the whole Psalter is prayed each week. Tradition informs us that earlier monks used to pray all 150 psalms in a single day. Benedict says, "Let us hope that we, lukewarm as we are, can achieve it in a whole week" (18:25).

Indeed, nothing should come before the Work of God, Benedict insists. The Work of God *(Opus Dei)* is Benedictine prayer. It has its origins in primitive Christianity. Paul urged the Colossians to encourage each other by singing psalms, hymns, and canticles. The first Christians, converts from Judaism, retained the prayers of their ancestors. Before the construction of public churches was allowed, Christians gathered during the night and day in private places to pray the psalms. The urban Christians prayed the psalms. So did the ascetics in the desert and in the early cenobitical monastics. Benedict considered the psalms so necessary that he encouraged his followers to memorize them in their free time. Monks traveling or working in the fields, when the hour for prayer arrived, had to stop and attend to the psalms. Although an oblate usually prays the psalms privately, he or she is united in spirit when the monastic community of one's affiliation is praying.

An elderly woman whom I'd just invested in the oblates told me that she wasn't going to say those prayers in the little book I'd given her. Instead she was going to pray several rosaries throughout the day. I told her the little book contained morning and evening prayer from the Divine Office. I tried selling her on the book because it featured the psalms. I emphasized, "These are the prayers Jesus said. He learned them in His childhood and prayed them in the temple and at home." That didn't matter to her, and I didn't argue the point. After all, she was the abbot's mother. Of course I could have told her St. Benedict never prayed the rosary. It had not come into use during his lifetime.

But do the psalms really have any relevance for Christians? Sister Irene Nowell answers that question in *Work of God: Benedictine Prayer*, a breviary and devotional book especially for oblates. "The fact that they are still kept by Jews and Christians alike is testimony to our common belief that God still speaks to us through these prayers. In the psalms there is a powerful joining of God's words to us and our words to God. We read them as God's word to us; we take the gift of that word, fill it with our own life's experience, and return it to God."

Not all the psalms are nice. Instead of praising God, some are expressions of anger. It seems difficult to pray when surrounded by so much violence and vindictiveness. How can a Christian be comfortable asking God to "blot out" someone? Shouldn't we concentrate on prayers of thanksgiving and make intercessions that are not so vituperative? Sister Irene suggests praying these psalms as "an acknowledgment that, left to ourselves, we would lash out against those who hurt us. Therefore we bring our anger and our frustration to God. We trust God to restore goodness to our lives because we know that we cannot." It's also been suggested that we direct the cursing psalms towards the devil and his works. Once when we revised our Divine Office, the cursing psalms were removed. Abbot Alan made the liturgical committee put them back in. All of human experience is expressed in the psalms. On some days it is likely that even the cursing psalms can be prayed with a certain amount of satisfaction.

Father Meinrad, who taught the Psalms to my novitiate class forty-five years ago, told us, "Make them your own." A recently invested oblate expressed to me her appreciation for the psalms. "One of the neatest things is praying," she said. "I've never disciplined myself to pray regularly before, and the first few weeks I was really rigid about praying the psalms. I started singing them, reading them out loud, standing, sitting, kneeling—just trying different ways. The best is sitting and slowly reading out loud, trying to feel the ideas and images with all my senses."

The Divine Office, the primary work of Benedictines, was developed over the centuries, but has been modified in more recent years. Besides the psalms, each of the offices has a short Scripture reading. Vigils or the office of readings has a longer selection from Scripture and a non-Scriptural reading. Monastic men and women once prayed eight offices daily, beginning very early in the morning with vigils or matins. Some monasteries still follow this schedule. Many other houses depend on morning prayer, noon prayer, vespers, and compline only. The Canticle of Zechariah is sung or recited at morning prayer and the Canticle of Mary at evening prayer. Here in my community, we have an office of readings instead of compline.

Oblates are encouraged (but not morally bound) to pray morning and evening prayer. Some oblates, though, pray more than these two offices of the Liturgy of the Hours.

One time I was the guest of a retired oblate couple who had the custom of eating supper in their pajamas and bathrobes. After the meal, they watched television until bedtime. But before turning on the TV, we prayed evening prayer. "Wouldn't you like to get into your pajamas?" the wife asked me. I presumed she was joking. Although when I was a student in a Benedictine college for men, we prayed compline, the night prayer, in the dormitory corridor, and some of the guys came in their pajamas. I told the oblates I'd rather not put on my pajamas.

Holy Reading

Besides praying the Divine Office, oblates are encouraged to follow the monastic practice of holy reading *(lectio divina)*. Reading was so important for St. Benedict that he had one or two seniors go through the monastery at the scheduled times during the week to make sure the monks were doing their reading. "On Sundays all are to be engaged in reading except those who have been assigned various duties" (48:22). I wonder what he'd say about monks watching the Sunday afternoon basketball games as they do nowadays in my monastery.

In the last chapter of the Rule, Benedict asks, "What page, what passage of the inspired books of the Old and New Testaments is not the truest of guides for human life?" (73:3). In the Prologue he says we will make our journey through life guided by the gospel.

We read the Bible for spiritual enrichment. The monastic method has been likened to a cow chewing the cud. The reader is expected to ruminate, chew over what has appeared in the text, and then find meaning or application for oneself. In Benedict's day, the monk devoted three hours to reading the Bible. Of the monks sent to check on the brethren during the times of *lectio divina*, Benedict says, "Their duty is to see that no brother is so apathetic as to waste time or engage in idle talk to the neglect of his reading, and so not only harm himself but also distract others" (48:18). Such a monk should be corrected twice and then punished if he doesn't reform. We had an old monk who was given an overstuffed chair for his room. "It's so comfortable," he told me, "that I have no trouble falling asleep during *lectio*."

Most modern Benedictine monks and nuns, because of the kinds of work to which their communities are committed, cannot afford to sit down with their Bibles for the long stretches of time provided by the Rule. Nor are there many oblates who spend three hours every day reading the Bible.

Lectio divina, nevertheless, is a custom that should be cherished, even if it means taking a Bible break of a few minutes during the day. Wanda, who used to run the donut shop in the little town near our monastery, could often be found reading her Bible when business was slack. She was doing *lectio*.

Reading the Bible and praying the psalms remain important aspects of Benedictine spirituality. Christians of various traditions can appreciate this. Although we may differ in other ways, the Bible and psalms are basic for all of us.

A Life of Work

St. Benedict, in his time, realized that monks could not spend the greater part of the day in the church praying the psalms. Nor could they reflect upon Scripture all day. They had to work sometime. There had to be balance in their lives. In chapter 48 on work he says, "Therefore, the brothers should have specified periods for manual labor as well as for prayerful reading" (48:1).

I met someone who was thinking of returning to the religious order to which he'd once belonged, but his age was against him. He was a social worker who felt over-burdened with work. I inquired if the job required him to do everything that he was doing. No, it didn't, he said, but he thought he had become a workaholic. I suggested that he strive for balance in his life, something that St. Benedict insists upon. Since he was now too old to return to the religious community of his youth, he might want to become an oblate of St. Benedict. It was obvious that he needed some order in his life and work—a rule by which to live.

Work for the first Benedictines was mostly the routine kinds of jobs people have in maintaining a household. The monks' work was confined to the monastery. Chapter 66 of the Rule indicates, "The monastery should, if possible, be so constructed that within it all necessities, such as water, mill and garden are contained, and the various crafts are practiced. Then there will be no need for the monks to roam outside, because this is not at all good for their souls" (66:6-7). Benedict says they should stay home and work.

Cooking, cleaning, repairing, gardening, and farming— this is the ordinary kind of work that is done in monasteries. Benedict calls our involvement with such work an expression of love. Whenever one of the monks tells me that I've prepared an especially good breakfast on a particular Tuesday, I reply that I did it out of love. Work should be done without grumbling, without sadness, and without being overburdened. Help should be given to all who need it. These are indeed fair employment practices!

Followers of Benedict's Rule, perhaps more than any other religious, place a high value on manual labor. A visitor once asked a confrere of mine the difference between this monastery and another that is better known than ours. "They're the scholars and we're the workers," replied the brother. However, once when I visited that other monastery,

I found the retired abbot mowing the grass in the cemetery. Kathleen Norris says, "I have seen well-known Benedictine scholars scrubbing the pots and pans, abbots wiping tables." Almost everyone does manual labor in a monastery.

Benedict and other monastic legislators believed that sufficient work was necessary in order to keep their subjects out of trouble. "Idleness is the enemy of the soul" (48:1), Benedict said. So even the infirm are given something to do that isn't very taxing. Everyone who is able has a work assignment. On Sunday, Benedict stipulates that monks who can't read or won't read should be given some work to do. Yes, on a Sunday.

There were no slaves in the monastery. Nor were there any monastic serfs in Benedict's time. His monks did not live off the labor of others. If they had to harvest their own crops, Benedict reminded them that they were really monks when they lived by the labor of their own hands. The artisans sold the work of their hands but were instructed not to become proud because of the income they were earning for the monastery.

Oblates cannot come away from the Rule of Benedict without having learned some lessons about work. Work for them has the same meaning that it has for men and women who live in monasteries. We are all encouraged to go about our work faithfully, cheerfully, and carefully. The tools and equipment used in our work should be treated with as much reverence as the sacred vessels used at the altar. An oblate who is a college professor told me that St. Benedict pricked his conscience one day. He was sitting in his office when it occurred to him that he should clean up the mess. The words of chapter 32, "The Tools and Goods of the Monastery," spoke to him: "Whoever fails to keep the things belonging to the monastery clean or treats them carelessly, should be reproved" (32:4).

Another oblate asked me what exactly he should be doing in order to be a really good Benedictine. My reply was that he needed to tend to his work and the saying of his prayers. That seemed too simple a reply, too ordinary. "All right, in Benedict's terms what does this mean?" I told him it had a lot to do with attitude. "How do you look upon your work? Are you lazy? Do you put off doing things? Do you do the best you can? Do you look for ways to improve your work?

"Are you faithful to prayer? Or do you neglect it? Do you put aside your work when it's time to pray? Are you praying when you should be working and working when you should be praying?" Ours is a balanced life of prayer and work.

A Life of Relationships

St. Benedict teaches respect for every individual. There are no favorites. A monk may be advanced if he proves worthy, but never out of favoritism. Everyone is equal in the eyes of God. There is respect for diversity in personalities, for different people's needs and weaknesses. Solicitude is shown for the young, the elderly, the sick, and even the difficult. We should look after one another. Wouldn't it be grand if these values or practices could be effective in every family, every congregation, and every workplace? At both your day job and at home?

Bishop Creighton Robertson of the Episcopal Diocese of South Dakota, and an oblate of Blue Cloud Abbey, summed up Benedictine spirituality in his diocesan magazine:

> The spiritual life for Benedict is not an errant idea. It is not something we do without thought, without concentration, without direction, without help.
> Monastic spirituality is a spirituality of love. It is a way of life, not a series of ascetical exercises. It takes persistence. It takes dedication. It takes a listening commitment to the human community. It asks a great deal more of us than a series of pious formulas. It asks for an attitude of mind and a style of life and way of relating that takes me out of myself into the mind of God for humanity.

Benedict's way of life is designed for ordinary people. No heroics are required. Just balance, moderation, and a lot of humanity. The Rule is written for community, but it works only when the individuals within the community put it into practice. So much of the Rule concerns the individual's relationships. St. Benedict teaches us how to get along with one another. We go to God not in isolation from other people but with a community, a family. So much of the

Rule is taken up with social relations. We learn by the good examples of others, and also from their bad examples. We see how far we have to go and how far we have come.

Seeking and Finding God
Today and Every Day

ST. BENEDICT HAD NO INTENTION OF FOUNDING AN ORDER.
"The reason we have written this rule is that, by observing
it in monasteries, we can show that we have some degree of
virtue and the beginnings of monastic life" (73:1). This is
how he ends the Rule. Any monastery wishing to follow it
has his permission.

By the year 800, though, there clearly was a religious
order. I know a Benedictine nun who was attending a
banquet with men and women of various religious orders

working in a particular diocese. Each person was required to briefly describe his or her order. The nun who spoke before the Benedictine sister said that hers was the newest order in the diocese and that the bishop had founded it. When my friend spoke, she said, "I belong to the oldest order in the church, and it was founded by a saint." Can anyone top that? Will something as old as the Order of St. Benedict survive beyond our present age? Although particular monasteries have come and gone over the centuries, the Order itself will very likely endure.

Why? Because God continues to exist. The Benedictines' job is to praise God. They will never be unemployed because their prayer is the work to which nothing else is preferred. Another reason for the continuance of Benedictine monastic life is that it is founded upon the concept of family life. What does Benedict teach regarding life in his family? Every person is equal in the sight of God, but authority is necessary. The persons in authority do not make excessive demands. They exercise moderation and know when to make exceptions to the rule. Every one in a family has a right to be heard, even the youngest. The Benedictines are like any other family. Members know each other, grow up together, and enter old age together. Individuals in a family vary in interests and talents, but all are held in respect.

"Listening attentively to our children is the best and most natural form of consultation," says Dwight Longenecker in his book on parenting according to the Rule. "Listening to them is difficult because their conversation is often banal and repetitious. But in granting them full attention we construct a regular form of consultation and maintain open channels of communication which are invaluable." The Revered David Robinson, a Presbyterian minister, has written a book called *The Family Cloister*. The chapters deal with applying the Rule of Benedict to family structure, spirituality, discipline, health, togetherness, and hospitality.

For oblates with children, Benedict is the model of a loving parent, knowing when to be firm and when to be lenient. What can be more ordinary and familiar than a family and its daily routine? Benedict says that the Lord calls out to us daily. Persevere wherever you are by embracing the routine of your daily life. This is how you find God now. Benedict tells us in the Prologue to the Rule, "the Lord waits for us daily to translate into action, as we should, his holy teachings" (Pro.:35). He quotes Psalm 94[95]: "If you hear his voice today, do not harden your hearts" (Pro.:10). Don't seek God elsewhere. Seek God now, right here, in the routine things that have to be done. Find God in the ordinary circumstances of your life.

Rita Tybor, an oblate of St. Bede's Abbey, Peru, Illinois, says she had a very realistic introduction to the Rule of St. Benedict when she became an employee of the monks. "I learned from the Rule by watching how it played out in day to day life, in the way the monks interacted with their coworkers and with each other. In the way they professed their lives to God. Thus, my understanding of monasticism was garnered from the simple routines of ordinary days."

"Running" According to the Rule

"DO NOT BE DAUNTED IMMEDIATELY BY FEAR AND RUN AWAY FROM THE ROAD THAT LEADS TO SALVATION" (Pro.:48), Benedict says in the Prologue to his rule. He also tells us that "we must run and do now what will profit us forever" (Pro.:44). In the next sentence he locates the place for this activity of running. "Therefore we intend to establish a school for the Lord's service" (Pro.: 45). It's all right to run in Benedict's school. If you aren't running, you aren't making progress. Although the course may seem difficult at the beginning, we have the guarantee that "as we progress in this way of life and in faith, we shall run on the path of God's commandments, our hearts overflowing with the inexpressible delight of love" (Pro.:49).

Benedict encourages us to rise from our sleep—our lethargy—and to begin the reformation (re-formation) of our lives. It is necessary to begin and to keep moving through this school, but to do so at a reasonable pace. At the signal for prayer, Benedict has us set aside what we're doing. Don't linger, is his admonition, but don't hurry frantically. Do all things in moderation—even the salvation of your souls. The Rule mentions certain obstacles we can stumble over while on our way through life: stubbornness, disobedience, and rebellion.

Although the Benedictine way of life is unhurried and calm, there are certain matters that Benedict wants to receive immediate attention. Whatever is scheduled should be done promptly. Get out of bed right away. Carry out the superior's wish immediately. Satisfactions for mistakes at communal prayer must be made right then and there. An apology for other mistakes should be made at once before the abbot and community. As soon as guests arrive, the abbot and monks are to welcome them.

Benedict does extend time in a couple of instances. If two monks have a disagreement during the day, they must make up before the sun goes down. The invitatory psalm must be said "quite deliberately and slowly" (43:4) at vigils for the benefit of the latecomer. Although he arrives just in time for the main part of the Divine Office, he has to take the last place in order to shame himself into amending. "Should they remain outside the oratory, there may be those who return to bed and sleep, or, worse yet, settle down outside and engage in idle talk . . ." (43:8). Come in even if you are late, he says.

If a monk arrives late for meals repeatedly, he may be made to eat by himself and, furthermore, his wine will be taken away from him. Being late is one thing, but Benedict doesn't want anyone eating or drinking before or after the appointed time. Sharing a meal is something done in common. It's a family affair.

Esther de Waal, commenting on chapter 43, "Tardiness at the Work of God or at Table," remembers the importance of serving meals on time. "It was particularly true in the years when I was bringing up small children who needed the sense of security that comes from knowing that things happen at the right time and in the right places." I recall how bewildered the monks were here when supper was served ten minutes late.

Benedict teaches us the importance of keeping to the schedule. Have you ever been at a home where Thanksgiving or Christmas dinner was delayed because not everyone had arrived? The tardy person is sometimes late through negligence and poor planning, not because of a flat tire.

For Benedict, tardiness means setting oneself apart from the community. Tardiness shows a lack of good order.

Benedict teaches us to stick to our schedules and to be on time. Throughout his rule, he teaches us consideration for one another, and he promises us "the inexpressible delight of love" (Pro.:49) as we progress along this way. Benedict speaks of running, but Augustine in his homily on St. John's Gospel says that if we've been awakened from sleep, we should get up and walk. "Perhaps you are trying to walk, and are not able because your feet hurt. Why do they? Have they been running over rough ground, spurred on by avarice? The Word of God has cured even the lame." No excuses, Benedict and Augustine tell us.

Esther de Waal says that by adhering to the advice in chapter 43 of the Rule she is not letting things drift. She is "totally present to whatever I am doing, present with awareness, and therefore with energy for whatever that place, that moment may bring me."

PART TWO

Benedictine Values
for Daily Living

Climbing the Ladder

Besides running, St. Benedict advocates climbing too. The spiritual doctrine of the Rule is contained especially in the Prologue; chapter 4, "The Tools for Good Works"; and chapter 7, "Humility." Chapter 4 provides the code of behavior that every Christian observes. Monastics and oblates, because they are Christians, are obliged to follow these seventy-four maxims that Benedict calls *tools*.

Chapter 7 is the longest chapter in the Rule. It is inspired by Jacob's dream in which angels ascended and descended on a ladder reaching from earth to heaven. The two sides of

Benedict's ladder represent the body and the soul. "Now the ladder erected is our life on earth, and if we humble our hearts the Lord will raise it to heaven" (7:8). We go up by coming down. St. Bernard of Clairvaux said it was more important to climb than to count.

If the beginning of wisdom is the fear of the Lord, so is fear the beginning of humility. Benedict spends several paragraphs emphasizing the need to be in awe of God. Our actions, Benedict says, are reported to God by the angels on the hour. That is scary! Having this sense of fear provides an incentive for developing right actions in our lives. Step one indicates that we should always keep the fear of God before our eyes. "Never [forget] it" (7:10), Benedict admonishes us.

Steps two and three require that we submit ourselves to the will of God and to another human being. The Rule was written for monks who make a vow of obedience, but other people are also obedient. Husbands and wives obey one another, children obey parents, and everyone is obedient to the boss. Monastics are asked to obey not only their superiors but also one another. Monasteries, families, and workplaces function so much better when subjects pose no threats of anarchy. Benedict holds out a model for us— Jesus who followed the will of His Father rather than His own will.

Obedience is often difficult regardless of our state in life and our form of employment. We see the flaws and inconsistencies in those people who ask our obedience. It is easier to exercise self-will without acknowledging any of our imperfections. In step four, Benedict tells us to persevere although the obedience may be to something "difficult, unfavorable, or even unjust" (7:35). On the other hand, Benedict tells the abbot of a monastery to rule reasonably and fairly. The monk who thinks he's received an impossible assignment may express himself to the abbot. Wicked abbots are to be removed from office or prevented from being elected in the first place. The laity living in the neighborhood are to be involved in carrying out this. Benedict would never approve of the kind of superior St. Thérèse of Lisieux once had—a Carmelite prioress who allowed the nuns to receive holy communion only after they'd each caught a mouse for her cat.

Climbing the ladder means, however, that we may have to accept a certain amount of suffering "without weakening or seeking escape" (7:36). Be patient, we're advised.

The fifth step asks that we confess our wrong doing and even our sinful thoughts to the superior. This is not sacramental confession. It's the ancient monastic custom of totally baring one's soul to a particular person. The desert monks and nuns all had a spiritual father or mother.

Alcoholics Anonymous has twelve steps, the fifth being: "Admitted to God, to ourselves, and to another human being the exact nature of our wrongs." I've heard fifth steps for a number of years, and often the person taking one will say, "I've never told anyone this before now." This is the kind of confidence Benedict is encouraging.

At this rung on the ladder, we may be discouraged from going any farther. Benedict is suggesting in steps six and seven that his followers humble themselves by accepting the "lowest and most menial treatment" (7:49) and consider themselves inferior to everyone else. In step six he says we're "no better than a beast" (7:50), and in step seven we're expected to admit that we're worms. Perhaps such attitudes are more in keeping with the mentality of the Desert Fathers, and have nothing to do with those of our present-day world. Nevertheless, these two steps can be climbed in order to discourage us from becoming arrogant. They apply to what Benedict said in the Prologue about people living by the Rule: "[They] do not become elated over their good deeds; they judge it is the Lord's power, not their own, that brings about the good in them" (Pro.:29). This helps to keep us humble.

Step eight of humility asks for conformity to the established practices of the house. Although Benedict acknowledges the individuality of those living in a monastery, he expects them to be conformists. If the inhabitants maintain the common practice there is no threat of anarchy. I know oblates who have used the dinner table as a setting for "chapter meetings" with their children. Work assignments—washing dishes and taking out the garbage, mowing the lawn, shoveling the sidewalk—were handed out for the week, things that needed correction (failure to do any of the above) were dealt with, and the children were given an opportunity to present their own matters for discussion. It was a household that operated smoothly because everyone tried adhering to the common rule.

The ninth step tells us in plain language to speak only when we're asked a question. The next step warns about laughing, and the eleventh prohibits speaking with laughter. We are to speak "seriously and with becoming modesty, briefly and reasonably . . ." (7:60). These three steps are concerned with the etiquette of speech.

In chapter 6, "Restraint of Speech," Benedict says, "We absolutely condemn in all places any vulgarity and gossip and talk leading to laughter, and we do not permit a disciple to engage in words of that kind" (6:8).

Don't we all become weary of hearing dirty story after dirty story? I suppose we also become tired of hearing about the scandal in other people's lives. What appears to be a prohibition against laughter is more difficult for us to understand. Oblate candidates are sometimes disappointed to find such a statement in the Rule of St. Benedict. When I was a novice it was explained to me that Benedict was speaking of buffoons. Benedict's intent here is to keep his followers from becoming buffoons. Some laughter is cruel and used in mockery. Genuine laughter is an expression of joy. Benedict is not condemning the kind of laughter that accompanies real joy.

The twelfth step indicates that we should not only be humble, we should also look humble. Benedict admonishes us to keep our heads bowed and our eyes cast down while sitting, walking, or standing. Nowadays, someone with this demeanor would be considered rather strange. It is not necessary to take on this appearance in order to be humble, but it is important to be humble—rather than arrogant.

Benedict concludes the chapter with the promise that by having ascended all the steps of humility on this ladder we will come to a love of God that dispels all fear. Speaking of the monk, but applied to all of us—monastics and oblates—St. Benedict says, "Through this love, all that he once performed with dread, he will now begin to observe without effort, as though naturally, from habit, no longer out of fear of hell, but out of love for Christ, good habit and delight in virtue."

Benedictine Ways of Behaving

ST. BENEDICT SAYS, "YOUR WAY OF ACTING SHOULD BE DIFFERENT FROM THE WORLD'S WAY" (4:20). I reflected on this once when I was riding in a car with an oblate of St. Benedict. We were in a residential part of town, and apparently he wasn't driving fast enough to suit the motorist behind him. She lost her patience and made an obscene gesture as she passed us. Even though this is the way of many drivers nowadays, I was surprised to encounter road rage in a small Minnesota town. My companion might have responded with an obscene gesture of his own, but instead, he blew her a kiss. "Your way of acting should be different from the world's way."

So often when something unpleasant happens to us, our response is to get angry. Benedict says, "You are not to act in anger or nurse a grudge" (4:22-23). This, of course, is sometimes difficult. Quoting Scripture in the very next paragraph of the chapter on "The Tools of Good Works," Benedict tells his followers not to seek revenge. "If people curse you, do not curse them back but bless them instead" (4:32). And this too is sometimes difficult. Jesus' instruction to turn the other cheek is one of the hardest things about being a Christian. As for the manner of treating someone engaged in road rage, however, one must be cautious. The kiss the oblate extended (rather than a curse) could have led to his arrest for sexual harassment.

When we react angrily or negatively about everything that happens to us, we're failing in patience. The Rule of St. Benedict refers to the virtue of patience several times. No doubt this is because monks are inclined to be impatient. He tells them to exercise the "greatest patience" when dealing with another's "weaknesses of body or behavior" (72:5). Things haven't changed since the time of Benedict. We still have to be reminded of the need to practice patience. People who live in monasteries get in each other's way. The officials of the monastery should be patient, St. Benedict pleads. No one should lose patience and strike one of the boy oblates. Neither should the monks strike one another. In the Prologue,

St. Benedict tells the monastic family that "we shall through patience share in the sufferings of Christ that we may deserve also to share in his kingdom" (Pro.:50). But we try avoiding people who either annoy or bore us. In the monastery, we call some of them characters. After the death of one confrere who had often tested our patience, an oblate wrote to us: "Your example inspired me to go out of my way to talk with him, to smile when I met him in the halls—and sure enough! Just as all the spiritual advisors tell me, our relationship developed and became friendship." The deceased had been a hypochondriac who staged "weak spells" that led to his collapsing on the floor. And he liked telling off-color jokes. Patience is required in living together in a monastery, in a marriage, and, for that matter, everywhere else.

St. Benedict wants the monks to serve one another without grumbling. He finds there may be reason now and then for legitimate complaints, but his goal is to establish a way of life that the "brothers may go about their activities without justifiable grumbling" (41:5).

One of my jobs in the monastery is to assign the monks to the duties of dishwashing and cleaning the refectory tables. Some of our monks are excused because of other pressing tasks. This is a proviso of the Rule. In our aging community with fewer and fewer new members, it's becoming more difficult to draw up the weekly list. "But I was just on," a monk may exclaim when the new monthly assignment sheet is posted.

It happens that a monk may do his duty without complaining, but his execution of it is done half-heartedly. We had a monk who was dismissed from cleaning the refectory tables because instead of washing the whole table, he only dabbed at the spills he noticed, leaving the ones that hadn't caught his attention. This was the same monk who emptied the refectory vacuum sweeper by throwing away the bag along with the refuse. Earlier in his refectory career, he'd vacuumed the carpet after meals for a whole week without ever having once turned on the switch.

I suppose most of us grew up in families where the children were required to set the dinner table and wash dishes. If there were enough siblings, the children could take turns. No doubt there were complaints over whose turn it was. Perhaps boys were even excused just because they were boys. Dwight Longenecker, the parent of four children and the author of *Listen My Son: St. Benedict for Fathers*, provides daily readings from the Rule of Benedict and applies them to ordinary family life. Regarding chapter 35, "The Kitchen Servers of the Week," he says, "Benedict's instructions that no one should be excused completely, and that the weak should receive help, reminds us that even young children can help around the house. If chores are shared they are more fun, and children can also understand that household tasks have a deeper meaning. Jesus served others; so we should too."

Jesus gave us an example of serving table and washing the feet of those with whom he lived and dined. In the monastery during St. Benedict's day "[b]oth the one who is ending his service and the one who is about to begin are to wash the feet of everyone" (35:9). We do this figuratively today, not literally. But what Benedict said still holds—the service we provide in our monastic families and in the families of oblates is done out of love.

Benedict believes that some chores are so important that the abbot and community should bless those doing them both before and after completing their week of service. This is a community ritual that is performed in church on the Sunday immediately after lauds. Here in our monastery we follow the rubrics exactly as they are give in chapter 35 of the Rule. Why does something so mundane receive all this attention? What deeper meaning could it possibly have?

The answer is simple: This is the Benedictine way of behaving. Benedict says we should all anticipate the needs of others and be fervent in our family commitments.

Peace and Justice

FOR A LONG TIME THE BENEDICTINES HAVE CLAIMED PEACE (PAX) AS ONE OF THEIR MOTTOS. Quoting Psalm 33[34] in the Prologue to the Rule, St. Benedict advises us, "let peace be your quest and your aim" (Pro.:17). Like all families, the monastic one also has its quarrels and squabbles. Benedict instructs the abbot to pray the Lord's Prayer aloud twice a day so that the monks may hear the words of forgiveness "because thorns of contention are likely to spring up" (13:12) in communal life. In the case of a major conflict in the monastery, expulsion may result if the troublemakers do

43

not respond favorably to counseling and prayer. Peace in the community has to be restored. Peace, however, is established through justice. Benedict is careful to arrange everything justly so that the members may live in peace. There are to be no favorite sons in the monastery; personal needs are to be equally distributed; special care is to be shown to the sick, the elderly, and children.

A few years ago, when I was the coordinator of the North American Association of Oblate Directors, I substituted for a speaker who was unable to keep his commitment at the biennial meeting. He was to address the subject of "Oblates as a Corporate Presence for Promoting Peace and Justice." In order to determine how my own community's oblates felt about this, I asked those who were at the spring retreat to respond to a questionnaire regarding their involvement in matters of peace and justice. It was obvious that they did not share a corporate presence, but I was amazed to discover how many were dedicated to various causes. Among these oblates were a lawyer, a minister, a retired college professor, a retired high school teacher, two nurses, a computer programmer, and a deacon. Their ages ranged from thirty-six to eighty-three. One oblate was a founding member of Bread for the World and the South Dakota Peace and Justice Center. Another served on the board of directors for an AIDS hospice.

I asked them if there were particular causes that deserved the support of Oblates of St. Benedict. A housewife and mother replied, "Anything that affects the heart and stability of the community: the poor, the sick, the infirm, the unborn." She worked for the Right to Life and Birthright. And she had demonstrated against pornography with people from Morality in the Media at an adult bookstore in her hometown.

In replying to what encouragement they received from the Rule of St. Benedict in the pursuit of peace and justice, an oblate referred to the Prologue in which Benedict says we'll arrive at the kingdom by doing good deeds. "We get there by our deeds, not words," she answered. "God's grace is not a substitute for activity. We have to awake, listen, and take action. Then there's the whole idea of conversion—openness."

Another oblate, after citing chapters and verses from the Rule, concluded by writing, "For me, one of the major attractions of Benedictine spirituality is hospitality—creating a safe place for everyone; feeding, sheltering, and visiting. The concept of peace is not just something interior but has a public dimension of working out the differences and disagreements among the people with whom we live and work."

On the other hand, an oblate stated, "I prefer not to engage in peace and justice issues because being an oblate is a matter of personal piety, not social action." One oblate was so disturbed by the whole notion that he went home and wrote an essay, "The Good Samaritan Was Not an Activist."

45

So, there is disagreement among oblates just as there is disagreement among those of us who live inside the monasteries. When our government was speaking of war in the autumn of 2002, we vowed Benedictines were offered the opportunity to sign this statement: "The central teaching in our 1500-year-old Rule of Benedict is that everyone, including every stranger, is to be welcomed as a blessing, and treated as Christ. From that stance of reverence for the other, we state our opposition to a military attack on Iraq." Not every monk and nun signed it, even though the document had been prepared by the Presidents of both the Benedictine Women's Federations and the Men's Congregations. Nor did a renewed statement in 2005 bear the signature of every monastic.

Not every monk and nun belong to Benedictines for Peace, an organization founded by Benedictine sisters in 1980 in response to the threat of nuclear war, and "revitalized in 1995 to network the Benedictine nonviolent response to countless areas of violence that threaten the world today."

One of the oblates replied on her questionnaire that, "Unless peace and justice are defined so broadly that no one could oppose them, you're not going to find corporate agreement among oblates. The reason for becoming an oblate has nothing to do with one's beliefs on social issues or the appropriateness of involvement." Nevertheless, when one makes oblation, there is a promise made, "to serve God and all people according to the Rule of St. Benedict."

A sixty-seven-year-old woman said, "Each oblate must decide for himself or herself—not as a group. Opinions are too diverse among the oblates." Oblates of our community continue to help carry the burdens of a diverse number of people including AIDS victims, street people, and prisoners. A Blue Cloud oblate has provided alternate health care in Africa and another has taught poor farmers in South America. Others have been arrested for demonstrating at plants where landmines are manufactured. One of our oblates crossed the line at the School of the Americas. Although it now bears a different name, this facility at Ft. Benning, Georgia, continues training counter-insurgency personnel from Latin America. Opponents of the school argue that the graduates are responsible for violating human rights when they return to their countries.

Living in peace and sharing it with others remains the quest and aim of all Benedictines. St. Benedict provides a model of Christian living for the Christian family and community.

St. Benedict, you were a man of peace. You walked the paths of peace your whole life long and led all who came to you into the ways of peace.

Help us, St. Benedict, to achieve peace: peace in our hearts, peace in our homes, peace in our sorely troubled world. Help us to be peacemakers.

Aid us to work for peace, to take the first step in ending

bitterness, to be the first to hold out our hands in friendship and forgiveness. May peace permeate our lives so that they may be lived in God's grace and love.

(Benedictines for Peace)

Hospitality

FATHER DANIEL, AT THE AGE OF NINETY, WAS ON HIS WAY TO THE FRONT DOOR FOR A WALK ONE SUNDAY AFTERNOON. Passing through the lobby, he came upon a young man and his mother. No one was attending to them, and Father Dan exclaimed, "Oh hell! Now I've got to do hospitality." Despite his initial reaction and response, he did the right thing. He took them downstairs and gave them cookies and coffee.

Oblate and Episcopal priest Elizabeth Canham says, "Being in the present moment is no easy task, especially

49

when we are interrupted by someone who needs our attention at a crucial time in some project. But attentiveness is what stability asks of us; this is how we express hospitality as we let go of what we are doing and pay attention to the person who needs our love." I like how she links these two Benedictine components: stability and hospitality. St. Benedict would have us be at home to welcome visitors "with the courtesy of love."

Very few people want to enter monasteries these days, but it seems more and more people want to visit them. On the other hand, there has never been a time—going all the way back to Benedict—when callers to the monastery were lacking. Once on the same day and at the same time, we had fifty grade school children and fifty senior citizens visit us. In the evening another large group arrived—oblates who had come for vespers and the monthly oblate meeting. The previous week I had helped conduct a tour and answer questions for a hundred college students.

People come here for various reasons. The college students were on a field trip. They were taking courses in sociology and anthropology. We offered ourselves as specimens of what they called an intentional community. "Is abstinence difficult?" one of them inquired. "From food or sex?" I asked. He was interested in knowing about the latter. The parochial school children were brought here to implant in them the idea of a religious vocation. I suspect they were more impressed with Gertie, our black Lab, than they were with any of us. Gertie was so impressed by the children that she boarded the bus with them for the trip back to school. The senior citizens were on an all-day outing with stops at several sites, including a casino. That same month a Methodist parish made a weekend retreat at the monastery, a housewife retreated for a couple of days during the week, an oblate spent some time in one of our hermitages, a Catholic priest got away from his parish for a few days, and so did a Lutheran pastor.

The Master in his rule claims that monks resent a guest who will not work. The Master is concerned about loafers and parasites staying in his monastery. Benedict's chapter on hospitality begins with the statement that all guests should be received as Christ. The Rule of the Master makes no such statement. Benedict imposes no time limit on guests nor does he put them to work. The Master gives monastery guests two days before assigning them work. If they refuse to work, they must hit the road.

Benedict, in the chapter on the role of the porter, places an older monk at the front door to greet guests. He welcomes them "with the warmth of love" (66:4) and asks for their blessing. Guests are a blessing to the monastery. Although Benedict is welcoming, he is also cautious. He warns about the delusions of the devil. Therefore the monks are to pray before offering the kiss of peace to a guest. No doubt both the Master and Benedict learned that not all guests were like those who called on Abraham and Sarah—angels in disguise.

When Timothy Radcliffe was the Master General of the Order of Preachers, he addressed the Benedictine abbots from around the world who were gathered in Rome for their 2001 congress. He told them, "Benedictine abbeys have been like oases in the pilgrimage of my life, where I have been able to rest and be refreshed before carrying on the journey. Everywhere I have gone, I have found crowds of people who were visiting monasteries. Why are they there? Some no doubt are tourists who have come to pass an afternoon, perhaps hoping to see a monk, like a monkey in a zoo. We might expect to find notices that say *Do Not Feed the Monks*. Others come for the beauty of the buildings or the liturgy. Many come hoping for some encounter with God."

Timothy Radcliffe believes that monasteries may be the only places in institutionalized religion that are free from suspicion in this era of secularization.

Everyone is so busy these days. Extending hospitality is often difficult. We're prevented from getting our work done. Or we have to be somewhere else very soon. We can spare only a few minutes of our time. To tell the truth, Christ often presents himself as an inconvenience in our lives. This is when monastics and oblates remind themselves that Benedict in chapter 53, "The Reception of Guests," tells us to greet everyone "with the courtesy of love."

Oblates everywhere can practice the same sort of hospitality that we practice in the monastery. Our community has oblates, a husband and wife, who never hesitate to practice hospitality. When Cesar Chavez's United Farm Workers came to town to picket the supermarkets, they were lodged in this home. A college professor and his family from India were unable to find housing at the beginning of the school year, and were invited to live with these oblates and their six children. A young man who had to leave his own home after having revealed to his parents that he was gay, was taken into this household. St. Benedict says, "Never turn away when someone needs your love." Around Thanksgiving time, the family clears out the garage and turns it into a pantry where food is distributed to poor people. It has been donated by some of the same supermarkets the United Farm Workers were encouraging customers to boycott.

A college student who dropped out for a semester and lived with us expressed these words of gratitude to the abbot: "Thank you for opening your monastic home to guests like me. When I reflect on the monastery from many miles away, it brings me back to myself and there is a great comfort knowing that whatever happens in the world, the monks are still working and praying, free of fear of the death and destruction so prevalent in the world. Thank you for maintaining a spirit and climate of loving kindness." Before he left us, he asked to be received as an oblate of St. Benedict. Hospitality is an heirloom of monks, nuns, and oblates. Benedict says we are to see Christ in our guests. We always hope they can see him in us.

PART THREE

Being an Oblate

Origins of the Oblates

CHAPTER 59 OF THE RULE OF ST. BENEDICT DETAILS THE
PROCEDURE IN WHICH PARENTS, FROM BOTH THE NOBILITY
AND THE POOR, OFFER THEIR SONS TO THE MONASTERY.
These young boys can grow up to be full-fledged monks.
Eventually, when they reached adulthood, they were given
a choice of staying in or leaving the monastery.

Benedict did not institute this practice of offering boys.
The custom of *oblati* existed in monasteries before he came
on the scene. He says nothing about the physical or mental
condition of the boys offered. In time, though, parents who

had sons with disabilities found a caring place for them in monasteries. The custom of child oblation in communities of men and women ended by the late thirteenth century. The Cistercian reform begun in 1098 was intended as a restoration of monastic life according to the Rule of Benedict, and the monks did not allow for boy oblates.

In iconography Benedict is often portrayed with two boys who had been offered to the monastery by their parents: Placid, son of Tertullus, a Roman aristocrat, and Maurus, whose father was a senator. Venerable Bede, the author of *The History of the English Church and People*, was taken to the monastery at the age of seven. In an autobiographical note appended to his classic work, he appears grateful to his parents for having provided him with a life in the cloister.

But when did adults begin offering themselves to monasteries without professing vows as monks or nuns? This took various forms and shapes beginning in the seventh century. There were groups of laity living in the vicinity who cared for monastery guests and for the sick and elderly for whom the monastery had become a hospice. There were also non-monks working and living in the monastery. Laypersons could become permanent guests, giving their possessions to the monastery in exchange for housing.

By the eleventh century there were two classes of adult oblates: claustral, those who lived inside the cloister, and secular, those who lived away from it. The custom of abandoning one's marriage partner and going off to prepare for death in a monastery became a pious practice. Here is an excerpt from a twelfth-century letter:

Gracious sister and beloved spouse, Odeline. For more than twenty years divine favor has allowed us to live with one another, but here I am leaning towards my end. . . . Agree to my desire to make myself a monk, renouncing all pompous attire of the world to put on the habit of the holy father Benedict. Lady absolve me from my conjugal obligations and, by your faith, let me give myself to God, that finally rid of the burden of mundane things, I merit the honor of receiving the monastic habit and tonsure.

This reminds me of a woman who recently at the evening meal informed her family that she was going to become an oblate of St. Benedict. Her husband, putting down his silverware, stared at her and asked, "Honey, this doesn't have anything to do with sex, does it?" The teenage son inquired, "Mom, does this mean you'll start wearing funny-looking clothes?"

The word oblate was first used to describe the people in secular clothing whose assistance Abbot William of Hirsau required in eleventh-century Germany. These oblates represented the abbot and community in worldly matters and on missions for which leaving the cloister would have been unsuitable. Oblates offer themselves to God and are often willing to offer their services to their monastic communities.

St. Henry, Duke of Bavaria, had wanted to become a monk in the tenth century, but the Abbot of St. Vannes told him to go home and fulfill the calling that was his destiny. He was crowned Emperor in 1014. His loyalty to the Benedictines and his observance of their rule earned him the title of Patron of Oblates.

The Patroness of Oblates is St. Frances of Rome. She was the mother of a daughter and two sons. After the death of her husband in 1436, she went to live with the society of women she had help found with the assistance of the monks at the Abbey of Santa Maria Nuova. These women, dedicated to serving the poor and sick, followed the Rule of St. Benedict without professing religious vows.

With monasticism's decline in the years leading up to the Protestant Reformation, there was also an abandonment of oblation. The new orders such as the Franciscans and Dominicans attracted lay followers called tertiaries. Rules were written especially for them, but Benedictine oblates have always adhered to the one and only Rule of St. Benedict.

It was not until 1904 that statutes and rules for oblates were formulated and approved by the Vatican. The oblates as we know them today can trace their origins to that event. The first American oblates were affiliated with St. Vincent's Archabbey, Latrobe, Pennsylvania, in 1894.

There was little interest given to oblates in this country until 1948 when the abbots of seven monasteries met at

Conception Abbey in Missouri to discuss what should be done to promote the Oblates of St. Benedict. In 1925, Abbot Alcuin Deutsch began a revival of oblates at St. John's Abbey in Minnesota, and other monasteries of men began enlisting oblates.

At that time, only communities of Benedictine monks could accept oblates of either sex. In 1942, a community of Benedictine women asked their chaplain to inquire about the possibility of receiving oblates for their own monastery. The chaplain, a monk, sought the opinion of an abbot. In reply to the chaplain, the abbot expressed doubt that the Holy See would ever consent to such a thing. Oblates would want spiritual direction, and it was not Rome's policy to put souls under the direction of women. One wonders if Rome had ever heard of mothers! It was not until 1961 that permission was finally given for women's monasteries to have oblates. Now, a person—male and female—may be an oblate of either a men's or a women's monastery.

The desire of so many people to become oblates has caused another group of monastics who follow the Rule of St. Benedict to consider having an affiliation of their own. The Cistercians call those who affiliate with them "associates" instead of oblates. The Associates of the Iowa Cistercians meet monthly at New Melleray Abbey (monks) or at Our Lady of the Mississippi Abbey (nuns) both of which are near Dubuque. Their Web site states that Christian men and women who feel called to a contemplative life style in the world, and who wish for it to be modeled on values found in Cistercian monasticism, are welcomed as associates.

Susan Stevenot Sullivan is a lay Cistercian of the Abbey of Our Lady of the Holy Spirit, Conyers, Georgia. In an article in *Benedictines*, she writes, "A couple months ago, I was asked by the novice master at the Abbey to pray for vocations among other things." It occurred to her that prayers for that intention were being answered, "but perhaps not in a way that many would have eyes to see."

Several years ago Abbot Thomas asked the Blue Cloud Abbey oblates to pray for vocations. Within a year, we had six novices. At an oblate meeting, he introduced them to the oblates. "Here they are. The answers to your prayers." As the year progressed, three left. The other three professed vows but are gone now.

Susan Stevenot Sullivan continues: "Who could have imagined dozens of empty choir stalls in the cloister and no rooms free in the guest house, or the possibility of affiliates or associates vastly outnumbering the cloistered professed?" They and oblates are the answers to our prayers, she says. "Those knocking at the door are male and female, single and married, rich and poor, Protestant and Catholic. Many have children, jobs, and rent or mortgages to pay." These are people who can't become professed monks or nuns. She wonders if this makes any sense to those of us who are permanent dwellers in the monasteries. I think it does. It all began with Benedict himself. His living in a cave for three years did not keep people from visiting him. They brought him bodily food, and in return he provided them with spiritual food. After he had ceased being a hermit and had established a monastery, we read of various people going there for physical and spiritual sustenance. "Never give a hollow greeting of peace or turn away when someone needs your love," Benedict says in the chapter on "The Tools for Good Works" (4:25-26).

Gerald Schlabach, an oblate of St. John's Abbey, writes in the *American Monastic Newsletter*: "Benedictines are hospitable. Monasteries do not turn away strangers. Monks do not turn away oblates. Yet Benedictines also do their welcomes discerningly, or should. And the oblate phenomenon, while certainly welcome, does require discernment." Monasteries require that a person not make oblation until a year after investiture. More and more monasteries are devising formation programs for this year of discernment. I know of one that will not accept oblates unless they live within a twenty-mile radius of the abbey. This is so the candidates may easily participate in the oblate formation program.

The writings of Kathleen Norris, Esther de Waal, and Norvene Vest have contributed to the increase in the number of oblates. Their work has especially inspired people from various religious traditions outside of Roman Catholicism. Kathleen Norris found in the Rule of St.

Benedict a model for living in a Christian community, and began applying what she learned from the Rule to her participation in the Presbyterian parish of Lemmon, South Dakota. From Benedict she learned about hospitality, prayer, and discipline. In fact, she gives credit to the Benedictines for making her a better Presbyterian. Sister Jean Frances Dolan, coordinator of the North American Association of Oblate Directors, welcomed the directors and oblates to the 2003 meeting by referring to oblate participants from many Christian faith traditions "who feel drawn by the Benedictine monastic charism and recognize themselves in it."

One doesn't necessarily need to affiliate with a Roman Catholic Benedictine community, however. There are monasteries in this country within the Anglican, Lutheran, and Methodist traditions. Some of them are clearly identified as Benedictine, but all are imbued with the spirit of Benedict. And all of them have affiliates. The Lutheran Benedictine monastery in Oxford, Michigan, welcomes all active Christian men and women as associates in the Fellowship of St. Augustine. There are oblates affiliated with the ecumenical Community of Jesus in Orleans, Massachusetts, where celibate men and women live in separate monasteries and married members live in their own homes. When I gave a retreat to the Episcopal Order of Julian of Norwich in Waukesha, Wisconsin, an oblate from the neighborhood joined his community every afternoon for the singing of vespers. This monastic order, founded in 1985, has both men and women as professed members. More recently a United Methodist woman has begun a monastery in Minnesota for women of her denomination, but the oblates affiliated with it are ecumenical. St. Benedict's Farm, a community of celibate lay Catholic men and women in Texas, has ecumenical associates.

The Oblate Forum is an ecumenical online community fostering discussion among oblates of many different monasteries in this country and abroad. Some vowed Benedictines also participate.

Over twenty years ago, the "Benedictine Experience" was begun at Canterbury Cathedral. Supported by an ecumenical group called the Friends of St. Benedict, this event is held at several places here in this country. Participants learn about Benedictine spirituality from monastic teachers while living a modified type of monastic life for a week. A Benedictine experience should include work as well as prayer and study. So, the participants undertake household chores at the facility where they are assembled. Some of these people are oblates and others become oblates as a result of having made a Benedictine Experience. As they return to their homes, it has become common for some of these people to organize cells within their parishes for the study of Benedict's Rule and its application to their lives.

In 2001 the North American Association of Benedictine Oblate Directors met at St. Benedict's Monastery in St.

Joseph, Minnesota. The event was co-hosted by the monks of St. John's Abbey. A panel of oblates from both communities spoke to the assembly about what being an Oblate of St. Benedict has meant to them. One told of how the Rule of Benedict inspired her to reconcile with a friend after a terrible argument. Another recounted how the monastic community had aided her in recovering from her husband's death. A single parent explained how she had learned to scale down her work in order to spend more time with her children. "Benedictine moderation and balance," she said. An oblate described how he and some relatives have established a communal home on a farm near monastery property. As oblates they pray together and live according to the Rule. At the end of the panel's presentation, a Benedictine sister in the audience commented to the audience, "After hearing these oblates, I feel like I need to shape up!" We learn from one another—professed men and women and oblates.

Susan Stevenot Sullivan maintains: "God knows who is a monastic. It is God who calls each of us to use our gifts for the good of the kingdom—however broadly or narrowly we perceive our vocations or how different those vocations may appear. It seems there are no effortless vocations, no greased slides into the next life, but perhaps there is something significant to be shared on the way."

The Reverend Mary McAnally, ordained in the Presbyterian Church and an oblate of my community, attended one of the meetings of the Association of Oblate Directors. In reporting the event in our Oblate Letter, she ended on a sad note "because of the disunity that existed in an otherwise perfect Benedictine bonding of Protestants and Catholics." This had been made evident by a sign in the vestibule of the church informing visitors to the monastery that only Roman Catholics might partake of the Eucharist. Although the oblate membership has become ecumenical, and Protestants have brought many blessing to the oblate way of life, there are, of course, still matters that separate us. Nevertheless, St. Benedict urges us to continue practicing good zeal. Even if we cannot sit together at the banquet of the Lord here below, Christ will bring us all together for the heavenly banquet.

I continue to be impressed by the oblates of my community who are such a divergent group of people from various religious traditions. Regardless of the differences among them and the restraints imposed upon them by my own denomination, we are all united in our calling to be Benedictine.

The Calling to Oblation

"THROUGHOUT THE AGES, THE RULE OF ST. BENEDICT HAS SERVED AS A SPIRITUAL GUIDE FOR COUNTLESS MEN AND WOMEN." The abbot addresses these words to the person who is making oblation in our community. Who were some of these men and women who had a Benedictine calling?

Thomas à Becket, with the blessing of the Abbot of Pontigny, is reputed to have worn a modified Benedictine habit beneath his bishop's attire. Thomas More was listed among the members of the confraternity of the Benedictine priory at Canterbury. Elena Lucrezia Cornaro Piscopia, the first woman in Europe to earn a Ph.D., was an oblate. (She'd wanted to study theology at Padua, but this was forbidden to women in the seventeenth century.)

In modern times, Dorothy Day, co-founder of the Catholic Worker Movement and advocate for peace and social justice, was an Oblate of St. Benedict. She visited here once, and I had the privilege of caring for her. When she left, I requested that she sign a copy of one of her books. She wrote, "For Brother Benet with grateful affection from a fellow Benedictine." The French poet and playwright Paul Claudel was an oblate. So was General Frido von Senger, the German commander at the World War II Battle of Monte Cassino. He was unable to protect the abbey from Allied bombing, but he evacuated the monks and had all the valuable art removed before the attack. When the Allies bombed this "Cradle of Western Monasticism" beyond recognition, the German general shouted, "The idiots! They've done it. All our efforts were in vain."

Philosophers Jacques and Raissa Maritain were oblates, as were the British actor Sir Alec Guinness and the American novelist Walker Percy. Senator Eugene McCarthy, a candidate for the United States presidency, is an oblate, and so was John F. Kennedy's mother, Rose. Many men and women who will never have any claim to fame have been and are oblates. Most oblates are ordinary lay people, but clergy may also adapt the Rule of St. Benedict to their way of life. Very few of the clergy who are affiliated with my own community are Roman Catholic. The wife and oldest son of one Evangelical Lutheran Church of America pastor are also oblates of Blue Cloud Abbey.

United Methodist pastor Richard Collman says of his visits to the abbey, "The monastery helps pastor the pastor. Without asking us to give up our own denominations, Benedictines invite us to share in their life together. They offer us places in their choirs, chairs at their tables, rooms in their houses, and rest for our weary souls."

When I'm asked to define an oblate, I simply say this is a person who loves what St. Benedict loved and who wants to practice what he taught. Sometimes I tell the inquirer that becoming an oblate is having a love affair with a Benedictine community. Unlike the affiliate of another religious order such as the Franciscans, Dominicans, and Carmelites, the Benedictine oblate is associated with a particular monastery of the Order of St. Benedict. This relationship with a single monastery is a distinctive Benedictine characteristic. Benedictine monks and nuns profess a vow of stability binding them to their respective communities for life. This vow provides a sense of solidarity in belonging to a family that dwells in a permanent place. A Benedictine monk or nun can visit another monastery where customs are familiar. He or she can even live there for a time, but it will never become home. Home is where one has made the vow of stability. The place for which one makes oblation is that person's monastic home.

The Reverend Richard Collman discovered this when he and his wife had returned to Blue Cloud Abbey after an absence of several years:

> We were sitting in the choir of the monastery, awaiting evening prayer, when the bells began to peal. Suddenly, I was overwhelmed with the feeling that I had come home to a special place and that my prayer roots were being fed once again by the communal prayer about to start. We had come for both a retreat and a friend's completion of the oblate process. I also would start the process of becoming an oblate, joining with hundreds of others who return to Benedictine monasteries around the world for the nourishment of their spiritual life.

I've heard members of Alcoholics Anonymous, who have been making retreats here for many years, also refer to the abbey as home—their spiritual home. Several of them have become Oblates of St. Benedict.

Esther de Waal, in the introduction to *Seeking God: The Way of St. Benedict*, refers to her returning to the Rule itself as a familiar place: "Sometimes one finds a place, a landscape, which is new and yet the forms, the shapes, the shadows seem already familiar. So it was with the Rule. It was neither remote nor past nor cerebral, but immediate and relevant, speaking of things that I already half knew or was struggling to make sense of."

A few years ago, a writer for *Time*, who was doing an article on the popularity of monastic retreat houses, called me and asked about the Oblates of St. Benedict. I told him people no doubt became oblates for the same reason they make retreats at monasteries. They want to partake of what monastic men and women have. Now and then I come across people who are disappointed because we monks don't reflect their image of monasticism. We're not medieval enough for them. "Good heavens! Don't you ever sing Gregorian chant?" Well, we do, but not as often as in the past. Other people may genuinely like us, but they're disappointed by our lack of enthusiasm for particular pieties and devotions. "What do you mean it's not the Benedictine thing?" Someone else may say, "Gee, I thought you'd be more like the Buddhists." A guest who spent two weeks here at the monastery was disappointed because he'd not had any mystical experiences.

An oblate's affiliation with a Benedictine community begins when he or she receives a medal of St. Benedict: "Accept this medal with its cross of St. Benedict and be reminded of the need to take up your own cross as a true follower of Jesus Christ our Lord." The medal we give is one that was originally commissioned by Conception Abbey for the celebration of St. Benedict's fifteenth-hundredth birthday in 1980. All of our monks received a medal. Ade Bethune, a liturgical artist and an oblate of St. Gregory's Abbey, Portsmouth, Rhode Island, had designed it. On one side was an image of St. Benedict and on the other a cross with the word *Peace* on it. The years 480-1980 were inscribed below. After the sesquimillennium year, the medal was made available without the dates, and this is the one that we use at an oblate investiture. When I went to the funeral of an oblate of Blue Cloud Abbey, I found her wearing my jubilee year medal in the coffin. When she'd been invested, I'd given it to her by mistake. I let Norma take it with her.

The person being invested is then presented with a copy of the Rule:

Accept the Rule of St. Benedict, written in the spirit of the Gospels.

Let it be your guide in life as a Christian and an Oblate of St. Benedict.

May it guide you in the way of Christ. May your concern for the needs of others continuously grow as you give of yourself to build up a true Christian bond with those around you: the strong and the weak, the wise and the unwise, the healthy and the sick, the rich and the poor, the joyous and those afflicted with sorrow, the lovable and the unlovable, the secure and the insecure, those well-cared for and those who are neglected, the young and the aged, those placed over you and those under your care, those of your faith and those not of your faith, whether in affairs of church, business, government, or any other area of life. May your study of this Rule inspire you to work zealously in harmony with others where you are, for the good of humanity and the glory of God. May God bless and guide you in your striving to be a faithful witness of Christ and St. Benedict. May God's grace protect you always.

A year after the investiture ceremony takes place, oblation is made. Oblates do not take upon themselves any of the canonical obligations that vowed Benedictines do. Oblates make promises instead of vows. Nevertheless, becoming an oblate is something that should not be done without serious consideration.

The Reverend Jeri Smith, a United Church of Christ minister, expressed in our Oblate Letter her feelings about being invested:

Years ago, when I first began coming to the abbey, I read the Rule, and was attracted to the Benedictine lifestyle because it seemed so sensible and comprehensive. It encompassed all of life; encouraged a sense of wholeness; and recognized moderation as a key to a full spiritual life. . . . When I heard Brother Benet read the words describing the tasks of a faithful oblate, I wanted to say yes, this is how I will try to be obedient to God's word.

Ideally, an oblate might like to live close enough to the monastery of one's affiliation in order to attend regular meetings and other functions. This is not absolutely necessary, however. What is important is to live in the spirit of St. Benedict wherever one's mailing address is. Oblate directors will keep in touch by mail. I know of one monastery that has a Benedictine On-line Oblate Chapter.

The Rite of Oblation

"Do not grant newcomers to the monastic life an easy entry," Benedict says in chapter 58:1 of the Rule. Do not let him in immediately. Test his spirits. Let him keep knocking, and if he's still at the door after four or five days, let him in partway. He may stay in the guesthouse a few days before proceeding to the novitiate. The longer he knocks, the more evidence there is of his sincerity. No doubt some would-be monks showed their lack of patience and left.

Oblates are not kept knocking at the door. Most oblate directors will encourage prospects to attend a few meetings before asking for investiture. I tell them to inform me when they feel ready. Some communities hold special sessions for such people before investiture. I knew an oblate director who stipulated a three-month wait while he inquired into the spiritual background of the one wishing to be received.

Some people who are invested drop out before making oblation. Others become disinterested after they've made oblation. Persons from distant parts of the country tend to lose touch. That's another reason why it's practical to become an oblate of a nearby monastery or one that a person can conveniently get to at least for a yearly visit.

In the ceremony of oblation, the person officiating (usually the monastery superior) reminds the candidate that he or she is already committed to Christ by baptism. Oblation may be looked upon as a renewal of that commitment.

The Rite of Oblation is modeled on the ceremony of monastic profession that is basically the same as the one described in chapter 58 of St. Benedict's Rule, "The Procedure for Receiving Brothers." Benedict says that the novice who makes profession should be aware "he is no longer free to leave the monastery, nor to shake from his neck the yoke of the rule which, in the course of so prolonged a period of reflection, he was free either to reject or to accept" (58:15-16). The oblate commitment is not this binding, but, nevertheless, it is still a commitment made after a period of reflection. Becoming an Oblate of St. Benedict is not the same as joining the Rotary or the League of Women Voters.

Chapter 58 instructs the novice to come before the whole community and vow himself to stability, faithfulness to the monastic way of life, and obedience. He reads his vows from a document written in his own handwriting, and then places it on the altar. In St. Benedict's day, final profession was made immediately after the year's novitiate. Now a vowed Benedictine lives under a period of temporary vows before making a permanent commitment. The oblate needn't wait so long. Profession and oblation both require the writing by hand and signing of a contract. The ceremony of profession and the ceremony of oblation have a legal and liturgical character. These are public acts done in the presence of the monastic superior and the community. Oblation is also a significant act even when made privately—as Frances Schmidt did in her own living room.

Vocal expression is given to the promises written by the person's own hand on what is called an oblation chart. Here in my community, the oblate stands in front of the abbot and reads the chart aloud after being invited by him, in the name of the community, to make oblation. "Peace! In the name of our Lord Jesus Christ. Amen. I (baptismal name) (oblate name) (family name) of (city and state) offer myself to Almighty God as a Benedictine Oblate of Blue Cloud Abbey and promise to serve God and all people according to the Rule of St. Benedict." The abbot responds, "May your oblation be acceptable to God and may your loving gift of self be eternally blessed." Then the chart is placed on the altar for signing by the oblate. It is left there until the end of the ceremony to symbolize the sacredness of the act.

After the praying of a short litany, including Our Lady of the Snow, Patroness of Blue Cloud Abbey, St. Benedict and his sister St. Scholastica, St. Frances of Rome and St. Henry, the patrons of the Oblates of St. Benedict, and the personal patron saint chosen by the one making oblation, the abbot concludes, "Compassionate and loving God, kindly bless all those you have chosen for yourself, especially all those who have associated themselves with our community. Strengthen us as we strive to seek you in all things and complete the work you have begun in us through Jesus Christ our Lord. Amen." Some oblates like to choose the names of Benedictine saints on this occasion, but this is not necessary. Any saint may be chosen or none at all. It's not surprising when oblates choose Benedict or Scholastica, but we do have oblates with Benedictine names like Cademon, Odo, Boniface, Dunstan, Ansgar, Anselm, Hilda, Gertrude, Mechtilde, and Walburga.

An oblate already named Dorothy as an infant took the name Dorothy in memory of Dorothy Day who is not officially recognized, but is indeed a saint for many of her admirers, myself included. "And she was an oblate," the other Dorothy reminded me.

Dorothy Day, who had made oblation at St. Procopius Abbey, Lisle, Illinois, lived poorly among the poor. She saw Christ in the poor—those who sought shelter and food at the Catholic Worker houses of hospitality. She was perturbed whenever anyone referred to her as a saint. "Do not aspire to be called holy before you really are," Benedict suggests. Dorothy was faithful in observing the Benedictine manner of life. In her declining years, she said that the beginning of each new day was difficult until having a cup of coffee and praying the psalms restored her energy.

Many oblates have looked to Dorothy Day as an example of faithful oblation. I asked Stanley Vishnewski, who went to the New York Catholic Worker in his late teens, and spent the remainder of his life there, to define what Benedictine influence there was in the movement. He replied, "Take away St. Benedict's ideas of hospitality, guest houses, farming communes, liturgical prayer, and there is very little left to the Catholic Worker Program."

Some years later at a biennial meeting of oblate directors and oblates, Brian Terrell spoke on "The Monastic Roots of the Catholic Worker Movement." He and his wife, Betsy Keenan, oblates of the Benedictine Sisters in Clyde, Missouri, have established the Strangers and Guests Catholic Worker Farm in rural Iowa. On the afternoon reserved for trips to places of interest, several of us directors and oblates chose to accompany Brian and Betsy to the farm at the edge of the town of Maloy. In his talk, Brian had said that he and his wife and children and neighbors received sustenance from their garden and their herd of goats as well as the production of crafts. This sounded very Benedictine to me. We were invited to a meal at Strangers and Guests. Everything served had been raised or grown on the farm. Before returning to Conception Abbey, the site of our meeting, we prayed compline. This, too, was Benedictine to the core. I'm pleased that five oblates of my own monastery are also Catholic Workers.

Why Others Have Become Oblates

Someone who was considering becoming an Oblate of St. Benedict told me that she had been advised not to get involved with the Benedictines because we're radicals. In my dictionary, the first definition of the word *radical* is: fundamental, basic. The second is: departing markedly from the usual, extreme. St. Benedict departed from the usual in order to restore what was fundamental.

Every reform movement in monasticism since the time of Benedict has been a return to the basic principles taught by him in his rule. And that rule, of course, is a moderate adaptation of the Rule of the Master.

The person who warned the prospective oblate about our radicalism was implying, no doubt, that we were far to the left of center. We Benedictines are sometimes surprised when accused of being so liberal. As the oldest religious order in Christendom, we consider ourselves pretty stable. If some people think we are far out, others may be inclined to think of us as being staid. The English word for radical comes from the Latin for root. We are deeply rooted in the past, and we must continue doing today what St. Benedict taught us long ago.

The person who labeled us radical was a Carmelite Tertiary, who informed our prospective oblate that she knew of a Benedictine community where, in opposition to the Roman Catholic Church, all the women wanted to become priests. I think she exaggerated. Had I been present

I might have informed her that even a Carmelite nun, St. Thérèse of Lisieux, "The Little Flower," regretted that she could never be ordained. And furthermore, St. Teresa of Avila, the other great saintly Carmelite nun, had been reported to the Spanish Inquisition because of her reputed unorthodoxy.

The Declarations of the Swiss-American Congregation of the Order of St. Benedict, to which our monastery belongs, state that a monastery "is a place where people from different walks of life and with different styles of thinking can find peace and inner renewal." The woman who was looking for an affiliation with a religious order chose us over the Carmelites. Oblates, like the members of the monasteries of their affiliation, differ about many things. But living together in Christ and caring for one another, regardless of our differences, is fundamental to Benedictine life.

Cathleen Curry, an oblate of our community, explains in her book on aging, *An Evening Walk*, what she found attractive enough about Benedictines to affiliate with them.

Once my children were gone from the nest, I had time to consider carefully my spiritual needs rather than just following the prescribed rituals carried from my childhood. The warm welcome of visitors to the monastery made me realize genuine hospitality was an important virtue in Benedict's eyes. His emphasis on stability, fidelity, moderation, and continual conversion to Christ settled in the low spots of my psyche, filling in the holes and smoothing out my path. As my grandchildren might say: "Benedict's your bag, Grandma!"

Lay people and clergy may choose the Carmelites, Franciscans, and Dominicans—among the older religious orders. Each has its unique spirituality, and the individual will approach the one that is most suitable for him or her. Carol Bonomo, who writes about being an oblate of Prince of Peace Abbey at Oceanside, California, started out as a Secular Franciscan. But she was advised to run, not walk to the nearest Benedictine monastery.

Will Derkse, an oblate in the Netherlands, is the author of a book describing how the Rule of St. Benedict may benefit non-Benedictine organizations. Referring to his personal attraction to Benedictine spirituality, he says, "I sometimes thought, if I had known this Benedictine world earlier, I would not have chosen marriage and public active life. I call this 'un-Benedictine' because Benedict is not interested in 'running away' from something to which you have committed yourself."

Kathleen Norris was an overnight guest in a Benedictine monastery when the Rule of St. Benedict was suggested to her as a good book to read in bed:

Written in the sixth century, a time as violent and troubled as our own, by a man determined to find a life of peace and stability for himself and others, it is a brief, practical, and thoughtful work on how human beings can best live in community. Its style is so succinct that it is sometimes taught in law schools as an example of how to say much in a few words. But the true power of the book, as with the Gospel it is based on, lies in its power to change lives. It has changed my life profoundly.

She became an oblate of Assumption Abbey, Richardton, North Dakota.

A few years ago, Norvene Vest, the author of a commentary on the Rule and several books dealing with Benedictine spirituality, spoke to the North American Association of Oblate Directors. She said that the oblate manner of life makes Benedictines known to the world. Oblates do this by their witness, their *conversatio*, their call, and their shared vocation. She sees monastics and oblates sharing a mutual blessing as they remain faithful to what St. Benedict called the rule he wrote for beginners.

Like all oblates and other people who get to know us, Norvene Vest soon realized that Benedictines who live inside their monasteries are not perfect human beings. "All the variety of human issues play themselves out in a monastery," she noticed. St. Benedict, of course, knew from

the beginning that we would have our struggles. Norvene
Vest understood that if the monks' home could be holy in
the midst of strife, so could the home of anyone else.
Referring to the abbey of her affiliation, St. Andrew's, at
Valyermo, California, Norvene Vest said:

> Over time, I have come to appreciate the true gift of
> the monastery to me. It is not primarily as a getaway,
> respite from my own struggles. Rather the Benedictine
> gift is the persistent aspiration toward God even and
> especially in the face of daily struggles. God meets
> me most reliably at the point of my temptations and
> self-doubts and discomforts. So reminders of my
> creatureliness are not causes of discouragement and
> despair, but are instead signs of deepening invitation to
> live in Christ's own life, just here and now. By the witness
> of their commitment to ongoing conversatio, the monks
> encourage me to believe in my own yearning for God.

When I came to the monastery forty-six years ago, I was
told that I was entering "the state of perfection." I wondered
what that meant because I saw so much imperfection all
around me. We no longer talk like that. Over my years of
living in monastic life, I have become convinced that St.
Benedict is the Patron of Human Imperfection. The
Benedictine—monastic or oblate, like a member of
Alcoholics Anonymous, claims progress rather than spiritual
perfection.

Let's admit it: monks and nuns are like other people. We are no better or no worse than anyone else. The oblates of our community have certainly discovered by now that we're not living in a state of perfection. All of us—monastics and oblates—need rules (or a Rule) to put order in our lives and to restore our lives to order when they begin falling apart. Benedict's Rule has the gospel for its guide, and it's tempered "that the strong have something to yearn for, and the weak nothing to run from" (64:19).

Like those rigorous ascetics before Benedict, there are no doubt people nowadays whose lives are more penitential than ours, and there are people who pray more often than we do. But for those who follow the course St. Benedict set, using the rule for beginners, we are all going to continue making progress.

Oblates know us monastics not only by our faults, they also witness our eccentricities and foibles. Kathleen Norris and I were once invited to tell stories about memorable monks and nuns at a meeting of the American Benedictine Academy. These "Monastic Tales" evoked stories from many of the monks and nuns and oblates in the audience. I heard the following story from an oblate before the professed member of the community could tell it to me.

There was an old nun who spoke not in tongues, but in malapropisms. She'd never had much occasion to leave the monastery for a social event, but the opportunity arose when she was invited to witness the marriage of a young relative. Upon her return to the monastery, she told the sisters, "They had a beautiful wedding in the church, and then went to the Holiday Inn for a conception."

Conversion and Stability

THESE ARE TWO UNIQUELY BENEDICTINE VOWS. *Conversatio morum* is often translated as conversion of manners and is synonymous with the vow of fidelity to the monastic way of life. This is not a once-in-a-lifetime conversion. It's ongoing. St. Benedict likes seeing people make the effort to change for the better. This means making changes in one's life, striving for something that hasn't been achieved in the past.

Benedictine monks and nuns vow themselves to conversion. Although oblates do not make a vow of conversion, they will practice this vow because they too are Benedictine. This means avoiding behaviors or habits that keep one from preferring nothing else to Christ. Conversion is concentrating on the kind of person we want to become. Merely entering a monastery or becoming an oblate, however, does not bring this about. There are no instant conversions.

Benedictine fidelity means being where one is supposed to be and doing what one is expected to do. Both the vowed Benedictine and the oblate remain faithful to prayer and work. Benedict is often misquoted; he did not say, "To work is to pray." Both are essential, but there are specific times for each. Don't work so hard that you can't find time to pray—that's more in line with Benedict's thinking. This is the fidelity to monastic life that is prescribed in chapter 58, "The Procedure For Receiving Brothers."

Conversion may mean changing one's mind, overcoming prejudices, looking at things differently. Someone has remarked that *conversatio* means never having to say, "But we've always done it that way."

Businesses have failed because management refused to make changes. Marriages have fallen apart because one or other spouse has refused to change, to pursue a conversion. Members of Alcoholics Anonymous tell one another their stories about what it was like, what happened, and what they're like now. These are conversion stories. Recovering alcoholics admit that God has done for them what they couldn't do for themselves.

Benedict says in the Prologue, "What is not possible to us by nature, let us ask the Lord to supply by the help of his grace" (Pro.:41). On the other hand, there is the reality that some things simply cannot be changed. After St. Paul's conversion, he was still plagued by a certain problem. He prayed three times for its removal. The Lord didn't take away that unidentified burden because Paul needed it for the sake of humility. In the Rule's chapter on good zeal, Benedict recommends "supporting with the greatest patience one another's weaknesses of body or behavior . . ." (72:5).

Does this get his followers off the hook? Should we even try changing our behavior or just learn to accept what cannot be changed? Benedict says some people have to be taken just as they are. We are to bear with them patiently. Nevertheless, he also encourages us to strive to become the kind of people we ought to be. "The Lord waits for us daily to translate into action, as we should his holy teachings." An opportunity for conversion occurs every day. But, realistically, on certain days, nothing much happens. Even so, it's expected that some progress is being made. Do not fret if you have not accomplished all you set out to do in one day, Benedict cautions. There will be another day tomorrow.

There is also a stability of place when one makes the commitment of an oblate. The oblate is united to a particular Benedictine family. There is also a stability of heart in the oblate's seeking God in the spirit of St. Benedict, loving the things he loved and doing the things he taught.

Benedictines promise to stay in place, to be committed to the monastic family in good times and bad. Our roots are sunk deep into the soil of a particular locale. One day in the post office I heard a neighbor ask a stranger to these parts, "Have you seen our abbey?" I was pleased that she felt comfortable in using the possessive pronoun. Monasteries are built with their occupants intending to stay in them permanently. This is why Benedictines make a vow of stability and why oblates are affiliated with a particular community.

It is sad when a Benedictine monastery has to close because of the scarcity of vocations. This is happening nowadays. A community of Benedictine women with whom members of my monastery worked on an Indian reservation in North Dakota had to give up when there were only six sisters left. I invited their oblates to transfer to our community. They chose to become oblates of Immaculate Conception Monastery in Indiana, the community that had made the North Dakota foundation on the Turtle Mountain Reservation in 1954. A former prioress of Queen of Peace Monastery stopped here on her way back to Indiana. She told us this was the most difficult thing she'd ever had to do in life—leave the site of her stability. Now, though, she was returning to the community in which she had made her original vow of stability.

People usually have good reasons for moving. Marriages fail, jobs take one to another location, and there are damaging situations from which a person must escape. Benedict himself left a community of monks, who'd asked him to be their abbot, and then they had had second thoughts and tried poisoning him. Several years later, he fled from the monastery at Subiaco because a jealous priest in the neighborhood was making life difficult for him. Benedict went to Monte Cassino, where he wrote the Rule, grew old, and died.

Stability doesn't mean that a person must never leave the house. Reasonable man that he is, Benedict knows there are times when a monk needs to take short journeys and long journeys from the monastery. A monk may find it necessary to transfer to another monastery or leave his monastery in order to become a hermit. These are clauses built into the Rule.

Benedict, however, had a good reason for insisting on stability in his rule. He didn't want any *sarabaites* or *gyrovagues* in his monastery. These are two of the types of monks described in chapter 1 of the Rule. The *sarabaites* have no rule. "Their law is what they like to do, whatever strikes their fancy" (1:8). The *gyrovagues* have no stability. "Always on the move, they never settle down" (1:11). Benedict prefers the kind of monks who have "stability in the community" (4:78), and not the wandering kind who make nuisances of themselves.

Stability, though, means more than sticking to one place. It's possible to live somewhere a long time—even in a monastery—without having much awareness of what's happening there. There are monks who never read the bulletin board. Someone may know more about a place than the person who lives there. We had a novice who was raised in Philadelphia and lived there until he came here. He'd never seen the Liberty Bell. It's good to know what's going on now wherever we live. It's also important to know where we've come from—where our roots are.

Stability most often puts us where God wants us to be. Stability means living in reality. Don't we say that someone who is not living in reality is unstable? Benedict seems to be telling us that we should be content with who we are, what we have, and where we are. Stability is a word that is synonymous with routine.

Sister Joan Chittister, in her *Wisdom Distilled from the Daily*, writes: "There comes a day when this job, this home, this town, this family seem irritating and deficient beyond the bearable. This is precisely the time when the spirituality of stability offers its greatest gift. Stability enables me to outlast the dark, cold places of life until the thaw comes and I can see new life in this uninhabitable place again. But for this to happen, I must learn to wait through the winters of my life."

Conversion and stability are inseparable. We are not just to be there (stability) but to do something and always try to do it better (conversion). "The workshop where we are to toil faithfully at all these tasks is the enclosure of the monastery and stability in the community" (4:78), Benedict determines. This is how he concludes the chapter called "The Tools for Good Works." Oblates don't reside in the monastery, but they toil faithfully in the places where they live, work, and pray. They employ the same tools used by those who live in monasteries.

Five Simple Guidelines for Oblates

IN 1971, A GROUP OF DIRECTORS PREPARED SOME GUIDELINES FOR OBLATES. These guidelines are common to every Christian. There are, however, certain attitudes and practices that clearly identify someone as Benedictine.

Oblates strive for their own continued Christian renewal and improvement. This is what St. Benedict calls conversion of life—*conversatio.* "As their states in life permit, oblates make use of various means for improving themselves spiritually, intellectually, culturally, and socially, by making a retreat, a day of recollection or renewal,

97

attending a workshop, seminar, or prayer meeting as occasion offers from time to time. They make the study and reading of Holy Scripture an important part of their lives, concentrating especially on the Gospel teachings of Christ." St. Benedict, of course, calls this daily *lectio divina*.

Oblates strive to be men and women of practical spirituality. "They combine prayer and work by living and working in the presence of God, aware of God's presence everywhere, knowing that God is nearer to them than they think. . . . They are patient and content with their lot in life. . . . They practice patience. . . . They are generous and warmhearted to the poor, the needy, the unfortunate, the sick, the sad, the afflicted, and the lonely. . . . They are concerned about the needs of others . . . . They faithfully fulfill the duties of their states in life, especially with regard to the care of their families and dependents. . . ." In other words, oblates use the Tools for Good Works listed by St. Benedict in chapter 4 of his rule.

Oblates strive to be men and women of prayer. "They strive each day to pray some part of the Divine Office, as the circumstances of their lives permit. . . . They strive to appreciate the beauty and spiritual wealth contained in the Psalms. . . . They harmonize their private and public prayers and devotions with the liturgical seasons and feasts of the year."

Oblates strive to be men and women of Christian virtue. The oblate directors highlighted the virtues of prudence, justice, fortitude, and temperance. All of these are evident in the Rule of St. Benedict. Clearly, these are the things St. Benedict teaches his followers.

Oblates foster a spirit of community. "They love the Benedictine community to which they are affiliated. . . . They foster the spirit of the community in their own family circle, and within the groups and organizations to which they belong." Here is what the directors said oblates could be doing for their monasteries: "They let others know about their monastic community, support its apostolic works, and encourage young men and women in their vocations to the monastic life."

These guidelines were written at a time when Christians from various denominations were first becoming Oblates of St. Benedict. The directors addressed this ecumenical character:

"Oblates strive to understand the religious beliefs and customs of others, look for teachings on which others agree with them . . . put aside all prejudice, and foster the spirit of universal brotherhood in God our Father." This is the kind of good zeal of which St. Benedict speaks.

The Value of Oblates
to a Monastic Community

AT THE 1997 MEETING OF THE NORTH AMERICAN
ASSOCIATION OF BENEDICTINE OBLATE DIRECTORS, held at
St. Meinrad Archabbey in Indiana, the following points
were made during a discussion regarding what oblates do
and may contribute to the monasteries of their affiliation.

1. Oblates bring a spiritual strength.

2. Because most communities are not growing by large
numbers, oblates expand the presence and participation of
the work and prayer of the community.

3. Oblates serve as a link between the religious community and parishes.

4. Oblates and the community provide mutual affirmation of the commitment to the Benedictine way of life.

5. The community is enriched by the interaction with oblates.

6. Oblates bring culture and insights (and experience in many areas) to the community.

7. Oblates remind the community of its goodness and uniqueness.

8. The witness of oblates living Benedictine charisms in the secular world strengthens community members' love and appreciation for the Benedictine way of life.

9. Oblates bring professional and personal talents to the community (most especially in an advisory capacity).

10. Oblates help spread the word of Benedictine spirituality.

11. Oblates help dispel myths about monastic life and help educate the public about the benefits/value of religious life.

The Benedictine charism is alive and well and growing because of the many people who are committing themselves to express this charism outside the cloister. I think this should make those of us who live inside the cloister feel more comfortable about our future.

The Great Gift of Oblates

Father Edward Vebelun, in drawing conclusions to his survey on oblates, wrote: "Oblates often speak with enthusiasm about the role of Benedictine spirituality and a particular Benedictine community in their own spiritual journey. The amount of attention to Benedictine spirituality continues to rise even while the number of monastics declines, so some suggest that the 'signs of the times' are calling communities to respond more generously in sharing their spirituality."

If oblates feel that monasteries are bestowing gifts upon them, Father Bede Classick, a former coordinator of the North American Association of Oblate Directors, sees the oblates as gifts to the monasteries and beyond:

Oblates are monasticism's gift to the world. I hope that through this statement all oblates will come to appreciate who they are. The oblates are indeed a gift and have much to give to the world, a world which is seeking and searching for its ultimate salvation. The oblate stands between monasticism and the world as a mediator, linking the two, drawing them together, bringing to the world the values which monasticism hold up as important for the Christian way of life.

In 1984 at the World Congress of Benedictine Abbots, it was noted that oblates receive blessings from the monastery, but they themselves are a blessing and support for the monastery.

At a regional meeting of oblate directors, a Benedictine sister reported that her community was now at the point where it could not function without the assistance of oblates. The oblates, most of whom live nearby, care for the elderly nuns and work in various offices of the monastery. I know of one community with a retreat house where the oblates make beds and clean rooms.

The world's abbots asked oblates "to continue steadfast in the way they have chosen, placing their trust in their Benedictine vocation." In the eyes of the abbots, being an oblate is a vocation, a calling. Notker Wolf, the present Abbot Primate of the Benedictine Confederation, acknowledged the importance of oblates by calling them to Rome in 2005 for the first worldwide conference of the Oblates of St. Benedict.

Phyllis Thompson, in an article published by *Benedictines*, acknowledges that the monks or nuns may feel intimidated by the oblates of their monasteries. As an oblate of Annunciation Monastery, Bismarck, North Dakota, she asks, "What happens if oblates, by their very numbers, seem disconcerting, difficult, even threatening? Do they incite fear or anger? Do some monastics worry that oblates are too vocal? The oblates might 'take over' or that some oblates—in their enthusiasm and zeal—appear to be taking over already? Do the principal occupants feel they are being edged out?" I have never asked my confreres how they feel about coming to the monastery refectory on oblate night and finding practically all the places at table occupied by oblates.

Phyllis Thompson goes on, "These are fair questions in an era where the members of most Benedictine communities are aging, where they are struggling to maintain apostolates, and where new candidates to monastic life are fewer in number." Eleven years lapsed before my own community had a monk profess final vows, but in that time over 150 people made oblation. Thompson points out to us monastics that oblates are the evidence that "a genuine desire for a deeper spirituality continues to attract many Christians to a 1500-year-old spirituality that they sense will nurture and sustain them in an era as chaotic as Benedict's was."

What was Benedict's charism? Unlike Francis, he wasn't a troubadour. Nor was he a brain like Dominic, a Doctor of Theology. Benedict dropped out of high school. Nor did he have the drive of that ambitious missionary and reformer, Ignatius of Loyola. Benedict was common, and the Rule of Benedict is ordinary.

In becoming an Oblate of St. Benedict, nothing extraordinary happens to a person. You won't be gifted with the ability to speak in tongues. You won't see visions. Your medal of St. Benedict (the one we give here is pewter) won't turn to gold. Life as an oblate is very ordinary.

Benedict uses many words to describe a monastery: a school, a community, a flock, a sheepfold, the house of

God, a rank of soldiers, a workshop, a tabernacle. Covenant is another image he uses just once: "How is it that you repeat my just commands and mouth my covenant when you hate discipline and toss my words behind you?" (2:14) This quote from Psalm 49 [50] in chapter 2, "Qualities of the Abbot," is applied to one who does not practice what he preaches.

Biblically, a covenant is when God makes an agreement with humans. "I will be your God and you will be my people." As we learn from the college students of sociology who visit here every year, a covenant is an intentional community of any sort. A covenant is not exclusive but inclusive. Benedictine oblates are Christians from various traditions and religious backgrounds who come together to form a covenant community.

Thompson suggests that vowed Benedictine men and women in these times will come to depend more and more on oblates. "Oblates and professed monastics must continue to be gifts to each other: Each community has gifts to offer the other."

Father Bede Classik ended his reflection on "Monasticism's Gift to the World" with these ideas on how oblates are the monastics' gift to the world:

The oblate today must be ready to walk in the steps of Jesus Christ.

The oblate must be ready to embrace the world in order

to forgive and heal and reconcile. Such a welcoming gesture will give others the courage to turn to Christ. Through the hospitality of the oblate, the monastic values of prayer, humility, obedience, peace, patience, charity, and reverence will be brought to bear on the world and guide it in the way of salvation.

Robert Rhodes, an oblate of St. Gregory's Abbey, Portsmouth, Rhode Island, in an article entitled "On the Vocation of a Benedictine Oblate" published in a 2002 issue of *The American Benedictine Review*, refers to the development of Christianity in Western Europe as "the permeation of the world by the monastic spirit." He says the oblate has an opportunity to be instrumental in the same way today. Isn't it remarkable that a sixth-century monk named Benedict can still have such influence in the twenty-first century?

Rhodes says:

In all the forms it has taken through time, the monastic spirit has been a sign of steadfast peace, order, gentleness, and tranquility. It has borne a quiet witness against the enervating luxury of the late Roman Empire, the political and social instability of the early Middle Ages, the restlessness and self-assertion of our own day. It is a continuing sign that the forces of confusion and dismemberment do not have the last word in history. It is this sign that we as oblates are called to appropriate and make manifest in the world in which we live.

What again are those signs of Benedictine life? Steadfast peace, order, gentleness, and tranquility. These are indeed good gifts to bestow upon one another and on the world.

Father Columba Stewart, a monk of St. John's Abbey in Collegeville, Minnesota, in his book on Benedictines, admits that we who live inside monasteries are gratified and amazed by the interest in Benedictine spirituality outside the cloister. He senses that our oblates and other friends of St. Benedict may have an even greater zeal than some of us: "What they may see more clearly than those in the monasteries is that Benedict does not pretend to teach other than the fundamentals of the Christian life. The Benedictine cloister's spiritual embrace extends far beyond its visible walls, usually much farther than those who live inside ever realize." It extends all the way to Frances Schmidt's living room in Dell Rapids, South Dakota.

There are so many people outside of monasteries looking in—seeking direction from a Rule of life that has guided monks and nuns since the sixth century. Benedict's Rule speaks to everyone. It was not written for individuals. It isn't a rule for hermits. For most people their fulfillment of the Christian vocation comes through living together. To all of us he says that it is all right to live comfortably—to be secure as long as we have worked for what we have, and aren't selfish or wasteful with what we own. Strive for balance, moderation. Put order in your lives, he tells us. Don't overeat. Don't drink too much alcohol. Don't even go overboard with prayer, but praise God every day and read your Bible. Be stable and content. Be at peace. St. Benedict did not write a rule for mystics. He wrote a rule for ordinary working people—people who are not caught up in the clouds unaware of those around them. The Rule was written for earthbound monks. It was written for a monastic family, but it speaks as well to the natural family.

At one of the biennial meetings of oblate directors and oblates, I heard one of the latter tell us directors to stop calling it "the oblate program." She said, "Being an oblate is a way of life, not a program." Is the Rule of St. Benedict really relevant for people living in the twenty-first century? Apparently it is. Benedictinism is common ground for everyone. There are in the world an estimated 24,155 Oblates of St. Benedict. According to the current census, there are 25,255 vowed Benedictine men and women. We are still in the lead, but the oblates are gaining. People from thirty-one countries attended the first World Congress of Oblates in 2005.

In Joris-Karl Huysmans's nineteenth-century novel *The Oblate*, a French abbot says, "We must resign ourselves to the conviction that the oblatehood of St. Benedict will never become widely popular; it will never appeal save to a chosen few. . . ." Oh, how times have changed, and how grateful we all are for having been called together by Benedict. "Are you hastening toward your heavenly home?" he asks us. "Then with Christ's help, keep this little rule that we have written for beginners" (73:8). Benedict prays that Christ will "bring us all together to everlasting life."

CONCLUSION

The Oblate's Prayer

Help us to become people of prayer and peace.
Though scattered far and wide, help us to be together
in the spirit of your love. Give us hearts wide enough
to embrace each other as well as those whose lives we
touch.

Enable us to listen and to learn from each other and
those around us each day. May we be models in our
homes, neighborhoods, and communities of wise
stewardship, dignified human labor, sacred leisure,
and reverence for all living things. Above all, O God,
may our presence among others be a constant witness
of justice, compassion, and hope to all. Amen.

(Adapted from the Alliance for International Monasticism
Prayer by Sue Walkoviak,
Oblate of St. Scholastica Monastery, Duluth, MN)

ACKNOWLEDGMENTS

Thank you, Lil Copan, for the pleasant afternoon at the coffee shop in Hingham where we talked about books and this one in particular. Thank you, Lillian Miao, for publishing the manuscript. Thanks to all the other people at Paraclete Press who have helped in various ways with the making of the book: Gail Gibson, Jon Sweeney, Ellen Ortolani, Jennifer Lynch, and Ron Minor. You have shown me gracious Benedictine hospitality.

SOURCES

Canham, Elizabeth J. *Heart Whispers.* Nashville, TN: Upper Room Books, 1999.

Chittister, Joan, OSB. *Wisdom Distilled from the Daily: Living the Rule of St. Benedict Today.* San Francisco, CA: Harper/San Francisco, 1990.

Classick, Bede, OSB. "Monasticism's Gift to the World," Newton, NJ: St. Paul's Abbey, December 2002.

Collman, Richard. "Full Circle," *Dakotas Connection*, March/April 2001.

Curry, Cathleen L. *An Evening Walk.* Notre Dame, IN: Ave Maria Press, 1999.

Derkse, Wil. *The Rule for Beginners: Spirituality for Daily Life.* Collegeville, MN: The Liturgical Press, 2003.

Esther de Waal. *Seeking God: The Way of St. Benedict*, Collegeville, MN: The Liturgical Press, 1984.

———. *A Life-Giving Way: A Commentary on the Rule of St. Benedict* Collegeville, MN: The Liturgical Press, 1995.

———. "The Benedictine Charism Today," Illinois Benedictine College Community, Lisle, IL: St. Procopius Abbey, April 26, 1995.

Eberle, Luke, OSB, trans. *The Rule of the Master.* Kalamazoo, MI: Cistercian Publications, 1977.

Longenecker, Dwight. *Listen My Son: St. Benedict for Fathers.* Harrisburg, PA: Morehouse Publishing, 1999.

McQuiston, John II. *Always We Begin Again.* Harrisburg, PA: Morehouse Publishing, 1996.

Norris, Kathleen. "The Rule of St. Benedict." *North Dakota Quarterly,* Fall 1990.

Nowell, Irene, OSB. *Work of God: Benedictine Prayer.* ed. by Judith Sutera, OSB. Collegeville, MN: The Liturgical Press, 1997.

Okholm, Dennis. "St. Benedict—Seeker of God." Academic Dean's Convocation, William Penn College, January 1989.

Purcell, Antoinette, OSB. American Benedictine Academy Convention. St. Meinrad Archabbey, August 2000.

Rhodes, Robert E. Jr. "On the Vocation of a Benedictine Oblate." *The American Benedictine Review,* 53:4. December 2002.

Robertson, Bishop Creighton L. *South Dakota Church News.* June 1998.

Schlabach, Gerald. "Welcoming Oblates with Discernment." *American Monastic Newsletter,* vol. 32, no. 1, February 2002.

Stewart, Columba, OSB. *Prayer and Community.* Maryknoll, NY: Orbis Books, 1998.

Sullivan, Susan Stevenot. "How Can This Be? The New Mystery of Monastic Vocation." *Benedictines,* LII:2, Winter 1999.

Sutera, Judith, OSB. "The Origins of Benedictine Oblation in the Research of Abbe Deroux," *The American Benedictine Review,* 52:1 March 2000.

Thompson, Phyllis. "Oblates—Stretching the Benedictine 'Tent.'" *Benedictines.* LV:1, Spring/Summer 2002.

Norvene Vest, "Monastics and Oblates: Mutual Blessings." North American Association of Oblate Directors, Conception, MO: Conception Abbey, July 1999.

Manual for Oblate Directors, Fourth Edition, 1993.

Handbook for Directors of Benedictine Oblates, 2000.

RECOMMENDED READING LIST OF BENEDICTINE TITLES

Benedictine Spirituality

Benson, Robert, *A Good Life: Benedict's Guide to Everyday Joy.* Brewster, MA: Paraclete Press, 2002.

Bockmann, Aguinta, OSB, *Perspectives on The rule Of Saint Benedict.* Collegeville, MN: The Liturgical Press, 2005.

Bonomo, Carol, *The Abbey Up the Hill: A Year in the Life of a Monastic Day-Tripper.* Harrisburg, PA: Morehouse, 2002.

———*Humble Pie: St. Benedict's Ladder of Humility.* Harrisburg, PA: Morehouse. 2003.

Casey, Michael, OCSO, *Living in the Truth: St. Benedict's Teaching on Humility.* Ligouri, MO: Triumph Books, 2001.

de Waal, Esther, *Living with Contradiction: An Introduction to Benedictine Spirituality.* Harrisburg, PA: Morehouse, 2004.

Earle, Mary C., *Beginning Again: Benedictine Wisdom for Living with Illness.* Harrisburg, PA: Morehouse, 2004.

Feiss, Hugh, OSB, *Essential Monastic Wisdom.* San Francisco, CA: Harper, 1999.

Norris, Kathleen, *The Cloister Walk.* New York, NY: Riverhead Books, 1996.

Plaiss, Mark, *The Inner Room: Journey into Lay Monasticism.* Cincinnati, OH: St. Anthony Messenger Press, 2003.

Pratt, Lorni Collins and Daniel Homan, OSB, *Living Benedict's Way: An Ancient Monk's Insights for a Balanced Life.* Chicago, IL: Loyola Press, 2000.

————*Radical Hospitality: Benedict's Way of Love.* Brewster: MA: Paraclete Press, 2002.

Robinson, David, *The Christian Family Toolbox: 52 Benedictine Activities for the Home.* New York, NY: Crossroad Publishing Co., 2001.

Tomaine, Jane, *St. Benedict's Toolbox: The Nuts and Bolts of Everyday Benedictine Living.* Harrisburg, PA: Morehouse, 2005.

Vest, Norvene, *Friend of the Soul: A Benedictine Spirituality of Work.* Boston, MA: Cowley Publications, 1997.

————*Desiring Life: Benedict on Wisdom and the Good Life.* Boston, MA: Cowley Publications, 2000.

Commentaries on *The Rule of Saint Benedict* Chapter by Chapter

Chittister, Joan, OSB, *The Rule of Benedict: Insights for the Ages.* New York, NY: Crossroad Publishing Co., 1992.

Kardong, Terrence G., OSB, *Benedict's Rule: A Translation and Commentary.* Collegeville, MN: The Liturgical Press, 1996.

————*Day by Day with Saint Benedict.* Collegeville, MN: The Liturgical Press, 2005.

Vest, Norvene, *Preferring Christ: A Devotional Commentary on the Rule of St. Benedict.* Harrisburg, PA: Morehouse, 2004.

Lives of Oblates of St. Benedict

Kulzer, Linda, OSB, and Roberta Bondi eds., *Benedict in the World: Portraits of Monastic Oblates.* Collegeville, MN: The Liturgical Press, 2002.

Divine Office Books

Benedictine Handbook, The. Collegeville, MN: The Liturgical Press, 2002.

Little Book of Hours, The. Brewster, MA: Paraclete Press, 2003.

Benedictine Daily Prayer: A Short Breviary. Collegeville, MN: The Liturgical Press, 2005.

Shorter Morning and Evening Prayer. Collegeville, MN: The Liturgical Press, 1987.

ABOUT PARACLETE PRESS

Who We Are

Paraclete Press is an ecumenical publisher of books on Christian spirituality for people of all denominations and backgrounds.

We publish books that represent the wide spectrum of Christian belief and practice—Catholic, Orthodox, and Protestant.

We market our books primarily through booksellers; we are what is called a "trade" publisher, which means that we like it best when readers buy our books from booksellers, our partners in successfully reaching as wide an audience as possible.

Paraclete Press is the publishing arm of the Community of Jesus, an ecumenical monastic community in the Benedictine tradition. We are uniquely positioned in the marketplace without connection to a large corporation or conglomerate and with informal relationships to many branches and denominations of faith. We focus on publishing a diversity of thoughts and perspectives—the fruit of our diversity as a company.

What We Are Doing

Paraclete Press is publishing books that show the diversity and depth of what it means to be Christian. We publish books that reflect the Christian experience across many cultures, time periods, and houses of worship.

We publish books about spiritual practice, history, ideas, customs, and rituals, and books that nourish the vibrant life of the church.

We have several different series of books within Paraclete Press, including the bestselling Living Library series of modernized classic texts, A Voice from the Monastery—giving voice to men and women monastics on what it means to live a spiritual life today, and Many Mansions—for exploring the riches of the world's religious traditions and discovering how other faiths inform Christian thought and practice.

Learn more about us at our Web site:
www.paracletepress.com, or call us toll-free at
1-800-451-5006.

Also Available from Paraclete Press

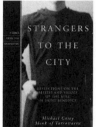

Strangers to the City
Reflections on the Beliefs and Values of the Rule of Saint Benedict
Michael Casey, Monk of Tarrawarra
ISBN: 1-55725-460-5, $15.95, Trade Paper

One of today's foremost writers and teachers of Benedictine spirituality shares the burdens of his heart for Christians everywhere. *Strangers to the City* is for all who are interested in deepening their faith through the dynamics of the monastic experience.

"Casey is a very good writer, and he makes the notion of monasticism something that can resonate with the common experience of us all. . . ."
—*Library Journal*

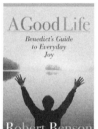

A Good Life
Benedict's Guide to Everyday Joy
Robert Benson
ISBN: 1-55725-356-0, $13.95, Trade Paper

Reflecting on what makes a "good life," Robert Benson offers an eloquent, warmhearted guide to enriching believers' lives with the wisdom of St. Benedict. Each chapter is shaped around a Benedictine principle and reveals the brilliant and infinitely practical ways that Benedictine spirituality can be applied today.

"Handy and insightful"—*Spirituality and Health*

Radical Hospitality
Benedict's Way of Love
Fr. Daniel Homan OSB and Lonnie Collins Pratt
ISBN: 1-55725-441-9, $16.95, Trade Paper

True Benedictine hospitality requires that we welcome the stranger, not only into our homes but into our hearts. With warmth, humor, and the wisdom of the monastic tradition, Pratt and Homan present a radical vision for a kinder world.

"A heartfelt sharing of stories, a welcome mat to enter into the spiritual discipline of hospitality."—*Publishers Weekly*

Available from most booksellers or through Paraclete Press:
www.paracletepress.com; 1-800-451-5006. Try your local bookstore first.